PARTNERING YOUR HORSE

PARTNERING YOUR HORSE

Susan McBane
Illustrations by Maggie Raynor

KENILWORTH PRESS

First published 2023

Kenilworth Press
An imprint of Quiller Publishing
The Hill, Stroud
Gloucestershire, GL5 4EP

www.quillerpublishing.com

Copyright © Susan McBane, 2023

The right of Susan McBane to be identified as the Author of this work has been asserted in accordance with the Copyright, Designs and Patents Act 1988.

ISBN 978 1 9100 1646 6 (hardback)
ISBN 978 1 9100 1647 3 (ebook)

All rights reserved. No part of this book may be reprinted or reproduced or utilised in any form or by any electronic, mechanical or other means, now known or hereafter invented, including photocopying and recording, or in any information storage or retrieval system, without the permission in writing from the Publishers.

British Library Cataloguing in Publication Data. A catalogue record for this book is available from the British Library.

1 2 3 4 5 6 7 8 9 10

Typesetting by SJmagic DESIGN SERVICES, India.
Printed in the UK.

The front-cover photograph by Paul Whitmore shows Lauren Whitmore, Dip OSSM, Dip ICAT, ESMI, with her horse, Flash.

The information in this book is true and complete to the best of our knowledge. All recommendations are made without any guarantee on the part of the publisher and author, who also disclaim any liability incurred in connection with the use of this data or specific details. The opinions expressed by the author in this book are her own views and may or may not be those of others.

CONTENTS

Before you Start...	9
Acknowledgements	15
Author Biography	17
1 Knowing Horses The Kind of Animal Evolution has Produced	19
2 What is Your Horse Telling You? Body Language and Recognising Well-being	31
3 Care and Management Really Matter Feeding, Housing, Bedding, Turnout and General Care	48
4 Tack, Clothing and Protective Items There is More to it than you Think	75
5 How Horses Move Naturally Why we Should Let Them	89
6 Co-operation, not Domination Riding **With** Your Horse, not Against Him	104
7 How Horses Learn And so, How to Train Them	121
8 Handling and Groundwork Good Companions	132
9 Flatwork From Going Backwards to Galloping	150

10 Jumping
   Forward to the Past					170

   Epilogue						177

   Books to Trust					180

   Help and Information				184

   Index						187

Before you Start...

I'd like to tell you what this book is about – why I felt it was necessary and how real partnership can be applied in practice to our association with horses.

The book is as much about attitudes and viewpoints as about horse-friendly techniques and principles. Many people, when talking about their relationship with their horse, often described as a partnership, are rather still thinking in terms of a boss/servant arrangement rather than an actual partnership. Much depends on how we have been brought up with horses and taught to think about them. We often think that we are providing the best of everything for our horse or horses, that they are living in luxury and have everything they need and want. But many of us look at things from a human perspective rather than an equine one: in other words, we don't really look at what horses want and need from **their** point of view but from ours – and this applies to not only their work for us but also their care and management.

The verb 'to partner' means to associate with or work together. So far as equestrianism is concerned, a horse and rider clearly do both those things. We sometimes come across the description of a horse-and-rider pair as being 'a true partnership' which gives the impression of there being equal status for both members in that partnership. Most people would feel that there has to be an upper hand on our part for safety reasons: horses are living and working in a man-made world. Some aspects involve being ridden/exercised on busy roads or being confined to a stable for many hours of the day with limited turnout, if any. There can still be a real partnership and we can secure this through horse-appropriate training and management techniques and the development of mutual trust.

There are also critical situations when a horse we are riding has taken charge and saved us both from a potentially disastrous outcome. It doesn't take much experience of horses, or even small ponies, for us to realise that equines are cleverer and more knowing than we have thought. They are very heavy, extremely strong, lightning reactors to anything they perceive as dangerous and, if really panicked, they can become uncontrollable to the peril of themselves and any person or animal nearby.

Can this really be the same horse or pony who nuzzles us for attention, gently mugs our pockets for food or just tags along with us as we poo-pick the paddock because he or she likes us and feels safe in our company? It's even more of a compliment when he leaves his friends and comes over to us, knowing very well that we don't carry treats in our pockets. How can such a big softy possibly turn into a potential, if unintentional, killer in a split second?

An ideal fit

The answer lies in the type of animals horses are. They are perfect examples of prey animals, food for others, and their almost instantaneous reactions to danger are what kept them and their predecessors alive and thriving for millions of years, before we domesticated them about 6,000 or 7,000 years ago. That is nothing like long enough to water down horses' evolved characteristics, which suit them perfectly to living in the open, in groups, grazing and browsing, and galloping away from danger.

Horses' long legs, long necks and heads, with eyes set high on the sides of the head, give a nearly all-round view. Their highly sensitive hearing along with the ability to rest and sleep lightly standing up enable them to spot and gallop away from predators in an instant. The predators may run as fast as or faster than their prey, but another priceless feature – horses' instinct to herd – means that only one kill satisfies a whole family of canine or feline hunters, leaving the rest of the herd to carry on life as normal. The herd members also rarely lie down all at the same time, there usually being one or two individuals left standing on watch to warn those lying down: it takes a sleeping horse about three or four seconds to wake, get up and start galloping.

The horse's brain does not immediately differentiate between a metal bucket dropped on the yard behind him, a bird flying into his face or a plastic bag about to grab his precious legs. It signals immediate danger! The horse's body floods instantly with 'alert' hormones while he mindlessly resorts to his first reaction – getting away. The flight-or-fight response is very familiar to horse people. Most horses only fight in defence when they can't escape something frightening but, because of their weight and great strength, this is their characteristic that is the most dangerous to us and we have to accept it.

(A few horses hide, if they can, or freeze when terrified. This is believed to be a remnant from the days when their early ancestors were forest-living, running away was barely possible and there was plenty of shrubbery and other greenery in which to hide.)

Working with what we've got

What has this to do with partnership? It means, firstly, that for both parties to be reasonably safe we have to damp down this instinct and control the horse's actions and reactions, as much as possible by means of **effective, humane training and conditioning** in our handling and riding. Secondly, it is obvious that rough, tough methods of dealing with horses will bring out the worst in many of them because they will be constantly on the defensive in our presence – not good or safe for either of us.

A situation has gradually developed over the past few decades in which a domineering and often harsh form of riding has become prevalent. At the same time, unsurprisingly, more horses are, I believe, put down for behavioural problems than ever before. Also, the general public, 'horsey' or not, is becoming increasingly ready publicly to object to and formally complain about perceived mistreatment. So far as partnership is concerned, horses do not respond favourably to a bossy, hard attitude. Modern rigorous research and studies have shown that they do not have overall 'herd bosses' of either gender to which the others must kowtow. Although individuals may have pushy or more laid-back characters, human-type hierarchies are not part of horses' social lives, as will be explained in this book.

There have always been bad horse people – rough riders and users, and also 'weak' ones who frighten some horses with their inconsistency, irrationality and lack of self-confidence but allow others to walk all over them. Conversely, there have always been special people who seem to have remarkably close relationships with horses, as though they understand them naturally, think like them and, using patience and gentleness (which is not the same as weakness) work wonders with them. This book will help its readers to work along the same lines.

Changing dynamics, economics and regulation

Until a couple of decades ago, research had been mainly in veterinary medicine but now there is much more rigorous work done on equine psychology and behaviour. This has revealed new knowledge of how horses really operate, think and learn, and has identified the most humane and effective ways in which to train and manage them, to the benefit and safety of our horses and ourselves.

Horses have varying personalities, like us, but one thing is known for certain now – they 'do' better for people who genuinely understand them, know what they are doing and do it with gentleness and confidence. The hard attitude that has grown in parts of the horse world in the past half-century or so is clearly misplaced and there seem to be several reasons for its worrying hold on equestrianism. One is the need of some humans to compete with others and show their superiority, using horses as their vehicles. Another is the changing economics of the work environment leading to the closure of many good riding schools that taught an older, kinder form of horsemanship.

Lack of basic knowledge and experience born of practical work has brought to the fore the natural, common human response to difficult situations, such as a horse seen as unmanageable or unwilling – and that is to get tough. Not knowing what to do with such a horse, particularly when the chips are down in a competition or stressful situation, many people resort to forceful, even brutal methods, which may create a violent reaction in a horse or, conversely, achieve short-term success of a sort but at the cost of the horse-human relationship and the horse's well-being. If it doesn't and happens again, the horse may well be on the road to the knacker's yard.

Worse is that this hard, 'big boss' attitude is almost the norm in much equestrianism today, even when the horse is not 'unmanageable' or 'unwilling', apparently employed all the time as a **preventative** measure. This is not horsemanship – it is bullying. Thank goodness it is not universal within our milieu, but I feel it necessary to get to the bottom of its development and pervasiveness in the horse world. I think the main reasons, apart from an excessive 'will to win', are the lack of good, general horse knowledge since the closure, usually for economic reasons, of many excellent riding schools and training centres large and small and the consequent lack of knowledge in people riding and associating with horses which leaves them unable to handle, manage and care for them appropriately. In desperation, they resort to harsh, desperate measures – and this does not only apply to relatively novice horse people. Those who want to make a career out of horses grow up and may be trained in these methods because former principles are often no longer understood. Teachers then often pass on this travesty to their clients who, not unnaturally, trust them and act accordingly.

Newer, scientifically proven methods plus the older, more empathetic ones based on long experience and the often daily association with horses enjoyed by previous generations can solve and prevent these problems – for 'ordinary' riders as well as household names. Learning how horses really think and learn, learning how their minds and bodies really work, and putting what they need and want on a par with what **we** want – that is the path to forming a **true** partnership with horses.

Susan McBane
June 2022

Acknowledgements

I want firstly to thank the publisher of this book, Kenilworth Press, for taking on its publication. This particular book, as stated earlier, is different from most educational or training-type books because it concentrates, at the root of everything, on our attitude to horses and the privilege of being able to own our own horse or horses or ride someone else's, either at a riding school or college, or in connection with our work if we work with them. Horses have been used by humans for thousands of years for food, sport, transport and any other activity in which their speed and/or strength could be of use to us. This inevitably led to their being regarded as tools or vehicles and generally being regarded as disposable.

Today, that attitude is no longer being tolerated by much of the general public worldwide. The UK government has only within recent years brought into law the fact that horses are sentient animals but that has brought to the fore the will to examine more closely how we treat them. We are hearing a lot now about our social licence to operate, or gain 'permission' from the public, to continue to avail ourselves of everything horses have to offer us.

Most books are enhanced by good, appropriate illustrations and I have had the good fortune to have several of my books graced by one of the best-known equestrian artists in the UK, known internationally, indeed – Maggie Raynor. It is a great relief to any author to know that their illustrations are in the hands of a supreme professional who also knows the subject inside out. As a classical rider and a horse owner herself with an excellent knowledge of equine biomechanics and psychology, she really knows her stuff, and I am grateful to be corrected by her when I get something wrong. I purposely chose to have this book illustrated only by her drawings instead of including photographs as well because you can show exactly what you want in a drawing whereas it can be extremely difficult to do so with photographs. I was delighted that she agreed to complement yet another of my books, so my most sincere thanks, Maggie, for partnering me in this endeavour to promote truly horse-friendly knowledge, attitudes and practices in all our dealings with a most remarkable animal – the horse.

Author Biography

Susan McBane is known worldwide as a long-established author, having written forty-six books, contributed to, edited and revised several others for publishers and written hundreds of magazine articles. She has an HNC in Equine Science and Management, is a Classical Riding Club listed trainer and Gold Award holder, and an Associate Member of the International Society for Equitation Science. (For information on both organisations, see *Help and Information* at the end of this book.)

In 1978, with Dr Moyra Williams, herself an author, clinical psychologist, sport-horse breeder and intrepid horsewoman, Susan founded the Equine Behaviour Study Circle, later re-named the Equine Behaviour Forum, editing its members' journal, *Equine Behaviour*, for thirty years.

Susan has edited two commercial magazines, self-publishing one of them – *EQUI* – and is currently Publishing Editor of *Tracking-up*, a voluntary, non-profit quarterly which she produces with three friends. She taught classical riding for twenty years, for most of that time combining it with equitation science, and has found the two schools of thought together to be the most effective and humane method of equine care and management, training and riding. She has also acted as an expert witness, consultant, peer reviewer, judge and speaker on equestrian topics.

I

Knowing Horses

The Kind of Animal Evolution has Produced

In this chapter:

- ❖ Horses are probably the most useful animals to man that ever evolved.
- ❖ Brief history of equine development.
- ❖ How the changing planet and climate produced today's horses and ponies, from forests to plains, and how this has formed them in mind and body.
- ❖ Why they do not all have the same characteristics.

Can you think of any other animal that has the same qualities as a horse and has been as useful to humans for thousands of years? In general, horses are strong, they are fast, they can jump and they are trainable: also, they are sociable with other species, they have excellent memories, they are adaptable within limits and they are intelligent, the gauge of intelligence being how well an animal survives in its natural environment.

There are downsides to the horse's complement of natural characteristics – they are very sensitive and, because they evolved as vegetarian prey animals, they are lightning reactors to anything that startles or frightens them, acting first and thinking later when alarmed. This latter quality plus their size and great strength makes them potentially dangerous. There is no getting away from it. There is no other creature which quite fits this description so well as a horse. They also have one prime concern in common with most other animals including humans – survival.

Evolution

The overall picture of the evolution of the horse family is a familiar one. It has taken about 50 million years for the horse we know so well to develop, in all its varieties, most of which were created very late in that time by man, intentionally and otherwise.

From a dog-sized, multi-toed creature living in forests and swamps, the horse's ancestors adapted by means of genetic mutations to the earth's changing climatic variations and environments. Some believe that creatures of all kinds can unconsciously place the stresses of living in a given lifestyle on their genes to change along with local requirements. Others prefer the theory that genes change or mutate, and are inherited, randomly, so if genes happen to mutate in a way that produces features which enable their possessors to cope with the changing environment, they will physically and behaviourally adapt to it. If they don't, extinction can result because their inherent qualities cannot cope with the new surroundings.

Whatever the method of mutation, the modern horse's ancestors did change to fit the environment on the different parts of the planet in which they found themselves. By the time recognisably different species had developed, the early 'primordial soup', as it is known, of around four billion years ago was long gone. The planet had developed different climates on different parts of it, as today, weather and seasons evolved and creatures of myriad different kinds thrived in the air, on land and in water, salty and fresh. The niche of the horse's ancestors was on land but in different parts of the planet with different climates, so those horses, if we yet can call them that, developed different characteristics to suit where they were – or, according to the other theory, those whose genes happened to have mutated in such a way as to fit the horse to survive in one particular weather/climate band did so and thrived.

All this means that, over the thousands and millions of years, the forested and swampy regions diminished and other environments appeared as well – plains, deserts, steppes, hot temperatures, cold temperatures, rains, snows, winds, earth movements and so on, and all points in between, which necessitated, one way or another, wide-ranging, different physical and mental characteristics to enable their possessors to live in those areas, survive, thrive, breed and become populous. (Today, there are 40 million donkeys in the world.)

Figure 1.1: The horse's conformation and biomechanics are ideally equipped for a prey animal that needs to gallop away from predators. The fastest gallop stride extends so that each foot travels and lands separately, so lengthening the stride. The stride is also lengthened by horses having no collar bone and shoulder joint as such, so the forelegs are free to extend further, creating a longer stride.

The fact that our horse's ancestors gradually experienced a diminishing number of toes until they are now down to one hard but sensitive hoof on the end of each leg, is slightly controversial. Some experts have said that this enables them to run faster but, considering that the fastest land animal on earth that may well have preyed on equines (and does on zebras, I believe) is the cheetah which has a full complement of toes on each soft foot, this doesn't seem to hold water. The single toe, or hoof, of equids represents the end of our middle finger or toe, the chestnut on the insides of the legs is probably a remnant of another toe and the ergot, that little horny projection on the lower, back of the fetlock, is likely another (as are the splint bones on legs), but there is apparently no evidence on the skeleton of this being the case. In both cases, they continue to grow and need trimming.

As well as changing feet, horse ancestors grew taller and developed longer bodies, legs, necks and heads, as well as long strands of hair for their manes and tails. Initially, ancient horses were forest and swamp animals and could easily find food all around. While multi-toed feet are an advantage in swampy ground, hooves as we know them are not, but as forests developed the fewer toes were not a disadvantage. It is postulated that horses developed the habit of hiding from predators among the dense shrubbery in forests rather than running away from them – difficult in a forest – and also that this could be where the skill of jumping (over fallen tree trunks) came from.

A change of diet, a change of features
Longer heads and necks helped to compensate for longer legs while grazing a new food that appeared – the grasses. Those legs were the key to the horses' survival while being hunted, enabling their speed to increase alongside that of the also-changing feline and canine hunters that were an ever-present danger. It was now that horses' instincts to flee rather than stand and fight, if possible, developed

and became their strongest instinct, the one we humans need to be most aware of in dealing with them. To assist in this, horses developed large hearts for their body size, super-efficient lungs and excellent air (chemical) exchange in their circulatory systems.

In a herd, it is very rare that all its members lie down to sleep or even rest at the same time. There is always a lookout or two remaining standing to warn the others of approaching danger, so that they can be up, on their feet and galloping away within a few seconds. To experience the most restorative kind of sleep they need to lie flat out but they can sleep lightly and doze heavily while lying balanced on their breastbones. Even standing up, they can doze and be off in a flash. While grazing, their long, thin legs are not much obstruction to large eyes set on the sides of the head near the top. This gives horses the facility of being able, with a small turn of the head, to see all around them to watch for danger yet feed at the same time, while their long necks also enable them to reach up and browse leaves from trees and shrubbery.

Horses' different types of hair also developed, either because of or incidental to the type of climate they were living in. The

Figure 1.2: In a natural equine family, consisting of a stallion, one or more adult mares and young stock, friendships between horses are close, particularly between mares and daughters. Young males are often sent away by the stallion when they become mature enough to mate – a natural way of avoiding inbreeding.

nearest we can get today to a truly wild horse is the Przewalski, native to Eastern Russia, Mongolia and similar regions. Like many equines, whether we would call them horses or ponies, that developed in cold, harsh climates, they have stocky bodies that hold the heat better than 'finer' equids, their manes and tails are of densely grown, coarse hair which also help in heat retention, and the fetlocks of horses living in similar areas are also covered in hairs, sometimes up to halfway up the legs. Horses naturally shelter from wind, and any rain or snow it might be bringing with it, by turning their hindquarters to it, so that their thin-skinned, sensitive areas between the buttocks are shielded from the weather. Some of these heavy or stocky types have manes that fall down both sides of their necks to retain the warmth in a relatively thin area of the body, while their rounded bodies can keep heat centralised within.

Compare the similar but different physical features of animals that evolved in hot areas of the planet. The typical hot-blood is what we call the Arabian but there is also the Akhal-Teke (a Russian breed) and the Karabakh, and other similar breeds. In recent decades it has been discovered, via genetics, that there is a good deal of, particularly, Akhal-Teke and Arabian blood in the most famous breed in the world, the Thoroughbred. The resemblance between some Thoroughbreds and, particularly, the Akhal-Teke, is unmissable. I had a wonderful Thoroughbred mare who looked like the full sister of an Akhal-Teke in an old book I had.

Horses evolved in hot climates invariably have thinner skin, thinner shorter coats, finer mane and tail hair, longer legs in relation to their bodies and, temperament-wise, are often 'hotter' or more easily aroused emotionally. The physical features are easy to account for. The thinner skin allows them to sweat more readily and lose heat that way, and to lose more body heat more quickly by means of simply radiating it out from their bodies. Their finer coats do protect their skin but barely obstruct heat loss from the body, although such horses can often grow surprisingly long winter coats, particularly if they are out a good deal. Not only, therefore, has evolution shaped them but also so can short-term environmental changes.

As for the psychological, mental development of horses, they developed as pure vegetarians and happened to develop, whether large or small animals, relatively chunky, meaty bodies which made them popular prey for carnivores. One equine carcase can feed a family of feline or canine hunters for days.

From our point of view, we need to recognise that this historic tendency is still very strong in domesticated horses and ponies today. It may seem unlikely to us, because they are not preyed on conventionally in domestic life, but **anything** that is unfamiliar, makes weird noises, moves quickly, particularly at ground level whether a dog or a plastic bag, or smells unfamiliar can instantly awaken the flight-or-fight instinct in equines. The quietest little pony to the most highly strung Thoroughbred can, without thinking, spin and gallop away, if possible, to preserve itself. If that is not possible, if the horse or pony is tied up, in an enclosed area such as a stable or small pen or (unusual in the UK) hobbled, it will fight with all its tremendous strength to get free. There is no thinking process in this. It is pure instinct and many an injury, to horse and human, has resulted from such incidents in a stable or other enclosed space.

If we are riding such an animal, and it can happen to any of us even if the chance is very low, we have to depend on the security of our seat in the saddle, on the possibility of our aids getting through to the horse and on the hope of bringing him or her under control as soon as may be. It has to be admitted that this may be difficult!

Applying evolution to management

This section is a brief rundown on dealing with what nature has given us, and will be dealt with in more detail mainly in Chapter 3 but also throughout the rest of the book.

The one thing horses and ponies do most of is eat. They evolved to eat for roughly sixteen out of twenty-four hours every day. They cannot help needing to do this but it is something most domestic horses don't get the chance to do unless they are on pasture. Yet this is an essential feature of their make-up and well-being and really has to be catered for if you want to be a friend and partner to your horse. Lack of this facility can cause a good deal of discomfort, distress and actual illness and pain in the form of ulcers in the stomach and elsewhere in the digestive system. I am sure it is a significant contributing factor to the development of stereotypical behaviours (formerly called 'stable vices') in mainly stabled horses.

There has long been the understandable belief that athletically working horses must be kept on restricted fibre (hay, haylage, grass) in their diet because they cannot gallop and jump with such bulky, roughage-type food passing through their guts most of the time. As well as adversely affecting their work, it would cause digestive problems with all that weight and fibrous mass in their

Figure 1.3: Horses spend most of their waking hours grazing but they still have to watch out for danger. Their eyes are set high on the sides of their heads, they have long, very flexible necks and their legs are thin and hardly obstruct their view, so they can still easily spot trouble all around.

digestive systems – a not unreasonable supposition. There are ways of compromising, however, without putting your horse at that kind of risk.

As humans, we tend to try to give our horses what we would regard as a comfortable home, as in a well-equipped and supplied stable, yet we know very well that a stable is far from a natural home for a horse and does not supply two of his three most necessary needs, and often not even the third one, either. Those needs are (1) tactile, social contact, (2) space and movement, and (3) enough appropriate food to keep him satisfied and occupied.

It seems that, because stabling has been the most common method of housing horses or keeping them under convenient control, for certainly hundreds and maybe even thousands of years, we now naturally believe that that is the right way to keep them. Just considering the basic evolution described above shows us that stabling, at least too much of it, is, in fact, a pretty poor way to keep horses.

Tactile, social contact: Most stables do not allow horses to touch each other as it is thought traditionally to encourage or even cause fighting, or at least make horses ill at ease. This can certainly be the case so the remedy is to only stable friends next to each other, or horses who at least get on with each other. It is bad horse management to adopt an old belief and keep friends separated because they might become 'too attached'. They will be much happier if they can not only see and hear each other (which is insufficient) but also touch, at least able to touch muzzles through 'chat holes' in their dividing walls but ideally going further than that. I have found that friends are fine with sizeable chat holes but if an even better facility can be offered that's all to the good.

Beneficial contact, of course, can be provided by turning horses out together either in pairs or friendly groups depending on the size of the turnout facility, whether that is on a surfaced area or in a grass paddock. It is very sad to realise the numbers of horse owners who actually want their horses turned out onto taped off, postage stamp-sized enclosures because they believe (a) that they cannot hurt each other and (b) they will be prevented from eating too much grass. This is not horse-friendly management.

Space and movement: Some horses are still kept today tethered in stalls, usually about 6 feet (a bit less than 2 metres) wide, facing a wall on which are containers for their food and water, with solid partitions between stalls and which are open at the front for easy access for grooms. It is amazing that some horses settle very well in such accommodation provided their other needs are met for significant numbers of hours every day. They can stand up, lie down, partly turn round and, provided also that they are worked, exercised and/or turned loose for several hours a day, they do very well and did so for many hundreds of years, usually in town and city situations.

Today, loose boxes are by far the most usual way of keeping our horses when 'in'. Size wise, for an average riding horse a box of 12 feet square (3.66 m) was traditional and many such are still in use, and many smaller, too. The above size is minimal, in my view. They obviously offer more freedom than a stall but full-time stabling, plus exercise or work, is not a fair way to keep an animal like a horse unless he has to be confined for veterinary reasons. The massive majority of loose boxes still do not provide for adequate social contact.

Adequate food and water: It has to be said that some horses, and particularly cobs and ponies, if left to their own devices would eat their heads off and make themselves ill – laminitis or 'fever in the feet' as it used to be called because of the feet becoming hot, is **very** common still, particularly in the latter category of equines, but any horse can get it. Excess amounts of feed and the wrong sort of feed for the horse or pony in question is the trigger so, in short, in order to provide a horse with enough food to keep him or her digestively comfortable and mentally occupied for something approaching sixteen hours a day and especially overnight, make sure your hay, haylage and, yes, the grass he grazes, is of a low-energy level. In this way, if the forage (the composite name given to hay, haylage and 'green fodder' such as grass and leaves from trees and shrubs) is low in energy but with all the balanced nutrients he needs, your horse can have a satisfying amount of bulk with adequate nutrition and still keep his head and his digestive system, not to mention his waistline, in good order.

Water is often considered the throwaway item in feeding our horses, but it is vitally important to most creatures. Horses, of course, naturally drink from ground level, their gullets being specially evolved to push the water up the oesophagus with the swallowing reflex and then down into the stomach. Therefore, where water is provided in buckets or containers, they should be fixed so that the horse drinks with his poll lower than his withers, otherwise he may well not be drinking enough which can cause him to be thirsty or even cause illness.

Applying evolution to training and riding

Anyone who has never encountered a feral or even semi-feral horse or pony (there being no truly wild ones left) can have no concept of how different their attitude is towards us from that of domesticated ones. We are so used to horses permitting handling, expecting food, being stabled, being turned out and brought in, being groomed, having their feet picked out, and so on and so forth, that it can be a shock to look one in the eye and realise that he or she regards you as an enemy or, at best, perhaps a source of food. If that engenders goodwill, it only lasts as long as the food does, then it is woe betide you if you don't depart at a rate of knots. Even foals born in domesticity are, in essence, wild, of course, for their first few hours. Skilled stud workers may apply a foal slip fairly soon after birth and give the new arrival a quick, once-over inspection, but then it is wise to leave mare and foal alone together as much as possible for about twenty-four hours.

Humans have been training, or schooling, equines for thousands of years, about 6,000 we think, and there have been plenty of horror stories of rough riders breaking horses' spirits because, in their culture, horses are still regarded as tools and vehicles – yes, it still goes on. Horses' natural inclination to flee in the face of danger, which is what these rough riders pose to them, is wrung out of them and they are worn down with all sorts of equipment, hard handling and riding, and so on until the horse gives up. Undeniably cruel and it should have no part in compassionate, enlightened horse training. Even in traditional, conventional training, the term 'breaking in' is still widely used, the preferable equitation science term for early training being 'foundation training'. That sounds much better to me, and it is.

The equitation science books recommended at the end of this book are the way to go as regards training, maintaining a mutually respectful relationship with a horse and, hopefully a loving and affectionate one. Most people, including me, feel that there is nothing wrong with 'using' horses provided they are trained and cared for humanely, which inherently means using methods horses' brains can understand. This is not, by far, always the case in conventional, traditional training.

Real classical riding and certainly the relatively new equitation science produce exactly the results you want (being reasonable about what to expect from your particular animal). They both take into account the evolution and natural nature of horses, and the techniques and practices given in this book, and in the ES books recommended later, take full account of the type of animal the horse is, and the individual characteristics of each one, principles much conventional modern riding often seems to have abandoned. Horses' personalities vary just as much as those of any other species depending on the genes they inherit, and we get better results if we work with them, at the same time using proven, kind, effective techniques.

2

What is Your Horse Telling You?
Body Language and Recognising Well-being

In this chapter:

- ❖ The importance of researching and thinking for yourself rather than just going with and doing what you are told.
- ❖ The latest evidence on equine body communication, and signs of emotions and health.
- ❖ Reading the signs, singly and in combination.
- ❖ Working with your horse's moods and suggested compromises, where necessary.

As our society seems to become more and more regulated, for well-intentioned reasons, we naturally get swept along with things like qualifications, registrations, organised bodies and representative societies. Along with the status that goes with qualifications and registration with official organisations goes a position of trust. When consulting such people we trust that we are in safe hands, that their advice or treatment can be relied upon to be appropriate and that we can confidently put into practice what we are told or advised to do.

Increasingly, it is becoming recognised that animals are not lower forms of life inferior to human beings as regards intelligence, emotions, communication, physical and mental needs, sensory abilities and all the other qualities that we humans experience. They are just as well equipped for life in this regard as we are and they are not inferior to us, just different, with senses and feelings adapted to their species to equip them to survive and thrive in often very different environments from those we put them into. Very many people know from instinct and experience that animals in general are very knowing, perceptive, rational in their own way and able to teach us a lot about themselves but about ourselves, too, if we will listen.

There is no doubt that they communicate in ways that can be both similar to and different from ours. Although they do not have spoken language in the way we do, they do come to understand different sounds we make as meaning certain things, just as we can recognise the meanings of sounds they make to us and other animals and the emotions expressed by those sounds. We can recognise the emotion behind specific animal sounds, such as a plaintive bark from a dog, a friendly whicker from a horse, a pleading miaow from a cat, and animals in turn know from noises we make (not necessarily words) whether we are angry, inviting, loving, happy, sad or whatever – safe to approach or best kept away from!

Thinking for ourselves

On the day on which I am writing this chapter, I have heard a story about a young rider and her pony, her mother and an instructor who was giving the girl and pony a lesson. Apparently, the pony was clearly worried about getting used to walking through water (a fairly common problem). In a nutshell, the situation reached the point at which the instructor told the girl to hit the pony to get him to go through some water. This did no good, but the instructor kept telling her to go on whipping him harder till he obeyed, which the pony did not. The instructor apparently said that if the pony was not obeying it was because the rider was not hitting him hard enough! (Remember what we said earlier about people getting tough when they're desperate.)

At this point, the girl's mother put a stop to the lesson. Later, she circulated what had happened among other horse people in their area to warn them about this instructor. She subsequently approached another, very skilled instructor who had earned a reputation for sympathetically helping horses and ponies having problems and, in one morning, the pony was walking, trotting and cantering happily through water, shallow and deeper, in company and alone, all because this second instructor had a real feel for him and, although being conventionally trained, had also studied other methods of dealing with horses. In addition, she has a real talent for what she does and great empathy with equines.

If this scenario sounds similar to anything you have witnessed or experienced, you are far from alone. So many people in influential, respected positions clearly do not even seem to like equines, let alone have any kind of real understanding of or empathy with them, but just use them for what they can get out of them, whether that is enjoyment, prestige, money or whatever else.

All we humans are fallible. It is also natural for us to continue in life the way we were brought up and educated or trained, and pass on our beliefs to our children, clients or pupils, perhaps our friends and others we come across in our work. However, this can be dangerous, or at least not the best way to proceed. A closed mind is difficult for other people to deal with and restricting to its owner. Yet we humans seem to find it difficult to change our ways, even though we know things would be better if we did.

Bearing all this in mind, may I suggest that you do not take for granted that everything you are told to do is the best advice. Of course we may want to consult other people who, surely, know better on a subject than we do, but some of these may be more interested in promoting their reputations than in the well-being of the horses. Our natural instincts and common sense are important and valuable to us, too. So far as equines are concerned, the fact that they are large, very strong and reactive animals is no reason to automatically treat them harshly.

If a trainer or teacher, for example, tells you to do something you feel is wrong, such as whipping your horse, hanging on to his mouth like grim death, kicking him hard especially with spurs on, forcing him to go in an obviously unnatural posture, or anything else that gives you that niggling little feeling inside that something isn't right, despite the teacher's reasons, be assured that it isn't right. You are right. Don't do it. Stop the session no matter what they say to you, who they are or where you are. The infliction of force, pain and fear, except in the direst of emergencies, are never the way to go and certainly have no place in a mere training session.

Understanding horses

If you think you do not have a natural 'feel' for horses but you like them, and do not associate with them purely for what they can do for you, rest assured that you can certainly learn to 'speak horse', to understand their body language and develop an inner sense for how they are feeling.

The main thing you need to do is to remember what kind of animals they are (Chapter 1) and put yourself in their position. Knowing, for example, that they need to eat for around sixteen hours a day and only sleep for around four to six hours out of the twenty-four, would you be happy or comfortable if your food ran out at ten in the evening and you were given no more till seven or eight next morning? If you had an object strapped around your middle which was uncomfortable or actually hurt you, with the weight of a human on top of it moving up, down and from side to side making it worse, would you want to get rid of it in any way you could or at least move in a way that lessened the pain a bit? If you had also something hard in your mouth pressing on firmly and moving about really uncomfortably or even painfully, would you be happy or even able to think about anything else but relieving your discomfort? These invasions of your well-being would become your immediate priority in life.

Other examples of many horses' lives could include being confined within four walls for most of each day and night despite being by natural inclination social creatures of the wide open spaces, being separated from friends and unable for most or even all of the time to touch them, having unwelcome things done to you by humans, perhaps being caused pain by them and not understanding why ... and many other occasions and practices in domestic life which are not generally geared to a horse's contentment or even welfare.

It is true that horses do adapt quite well to the sort of lifestyle we create for them, but few of us can doubt the difference in a horse's demeanour when he is given freedom with friends and as much food as he can eat. One of my favourite occupations for sheer relaxation is watching horses out together, nuzzling, grazing, rolling, playing, sleeping, scratching and doing all the things they naturally do when free. They ooze happiness and contentment, particularly when in a settled group of familiar companions. This is the best way to open-mindedly observe equine behaviour unless you have access to feral or semi-feral horses or ponies.

Watch them without judging them, and once you have the feel of a herd of family or friends together and make a habit of absorbing everything about their lives together, I think you'll find that it really makes you think about the things we do with them in domestic life. The two situations – nature and domesticity – can be poles apart. Horses can be very happy in the life we arrange for them, but we should make our mantra 'all things in moderation'. Being stabled for nearly all their time is not the best way to keep most horses. Being worked hard in ways that are uncomfortable and maybe painful, and for reasons outside a horse's ken, is unnecessary and not horse-friendly, and denying horses the close, tactile contact with and company of their friends when we know very well that they are happier when with them is not kind. There **are** ways of keeping horses fairly conventionally and also making them contented and, so far as we know, happy.

Before we continue with ways of doing this, we need to know, from observation and 'feel' or sense, how horses are feeling and the most obvious way of doing this is by understanding their body language. A 'deeper' way is to just **be** with them and open yourself up to anything they may be giving out emotionally, thinking about the horse rather than yourself, or just thinking about nothing and seeing what turns up.

Body language

Horses communicate mostly by means of body language and this language can be very subtle and complex, but that doesn't mean we can't learn it. Many people still do not connect with their horses because they do not understand, or they **misunderstand**, what their horse is trying to communicate to them or often don't realise that he is trying to communicate at all, so it all sweeps past their awareness, let alone their comprehension, and the horse finds himself talking to someone who is ignoring him. How frustrating, upsetting and worrying this must be, as we'll know if we have ever been ignored ourselves.

Humans, like other animals, have differing talents and abilities. Many people are really tuned in to animals, and know what they are trying to say to us and how they are feeling but some do not have this ability. They don't understand or speak Equus, or even realise it is possible – but it **is** possible and can be learnt. It might be rather mechanical by visual observation at first rather than sensing feelings, until the horse's emotions start to sink into their consciousness and they find that they **can** understand them and work on their wavelength. This must be a light-bulb moment for them, and a massive relief to their horses.

It seems to me that this aspect of relating to horses is not featured enough, if at all, in the training of conventional instructors, yet it is crucially important. It is also the case that, once qualified, an awful lot of people do not keep up to date with important developments in their field, equestrian or otherwise, and continue to pass on outdated, inappropriate information and advice to their clients or students.

The nitty-gritty

I'll describe individual, separate features first that denote particular emotions and then put some together and explain some combined features and what they mean. Horses' heads and faces are extremely expressive but they are backed up by body postures and tail positions and actions. Let's talk about the head and face first.

Starting with the ears, most of us know that ears forward or 'pricked' means the horse is paying attention to something in front of him, good or bad, so it can mean interest, fear or various points in between. Ears to the sides generally mean relaxation, sleepiness, resting or boredom, feeling a bit off-colour or actually ill. Ears softly backwards means that the horse is paying attention to something behind his head, either his rider or something non-frightening behind him whether an object, a horse, dog or person, or a noise. Ears pressed hard back denote distress, anger, considerable pain or difficulty, alarm and fear. Ears also are often positioned individually, such as one forward and one to the side, and indicate that the horse is thinking of two things at once.

Figure 2.1: A horse feeling good and healthy in himself will often be alert, bright and interested in his surroundings. His eyes will be bright and his coat smooth and have a sheen.

A lot of ridden horses today, with the modern harsher style of riding and hard, blocking bit contact, can be seen going along with their ears hard back and people think the horse is paying attention to his rider, which is what they want. In fact, the horse is expressing distress as in pain and/or anger – pain possibly from over-firm bit or spur contact or anger due to being forced by harsh aids into an inappropriate posture which is causing him severe discomfort or even pain and feeling unable to escape his situation.

An unmistakable example of an angry, aggressive horse is with the head stretched out towards a person or other animal he dislikes, ears hard back, eyes well open, nostrils wrinkled up and back and lips apart with teeth showing, saying very clearly: 'Get away from me or I'll have you!'. The eyes, traditionally regarded as 'the mirror of the soul', certainly in humans and why not in animals as well, can tell us a lot. An open, rounded, eye, bright and interested, calm or excited and all points in between, tells us that the horse is fine. When a horse is concerned and worried about anything the surrounding tissues of the eye take on a triangular shape. When he is feeling ill the eyes may appear 'sunken', dull and smaller than usual, which also can happen when he is bored, over-confined, lonely, deprived and generally unhappy. Some horses show the whites of the eyes more than others, depending on the eye conformation. Wide open eyes with the whites showing generally mean alarm and fear. People often think that obvious whites mean anger and aggression but this is not necessarily so.

The horse's muzzle is very expressive, too. The nostrils show various feelings. If rounded and opened it can mean excitement, alarm or aggression. Nostrils wrinkled up and back indicate dislike, distress and/or pain. Soft, half-closed nostrils indicate relaxation, sleepiness, tiredness, calmness, feeling unwell, bored, unhappy or resigned. The mouth held partly open, particularly if the lips are drawn back somewhat and the teeth showing can indicate considerable discomfort or pain in the mouth. A triangular appearance of the chin, likewise, indicates an unhappy, worried horse.

The horse's tail can give us a good deal of information about his feelings. It is, of course, an extension of the spine, with its own vertebrae and muscles, and can be most expressive. In a comfortable, relaxed horse, it will hang relaxed between the buttocks. In an engaged horse observing his environment it will be slightly raised and in an excited, very happy, playful or alarmed horse it will be arched. If the horse is frightened the dock will be clamped between the buttocks and in an angry or distressed horse it will be thrashed (rather than just swished) quite forcefully. When a horse is being ridden and his dock is stiff or, possibly, held to one side, it indicates a troubled horse, not happy with the way he is being ridden – and if the dock is stiff the back is stiff, rather than swinging with his movement. Conversely, if the dock itself, not just the long, free hair below it, is relaxed and swinging from side to side with the horse's motion, so will be his back, indicating a comfortable horse moving well.

Body postures and demeanours can tell us immediately on looking at a horse how he is feeling. Taking into account the above descriptions, the tension of a horse's skin can tell us a lot. In a healthy, contented, relaxed or happy horse you can place the flat of your hand on his ribcage and easily move the skin over it. In any other emotion, or combination of emotions, the horse's skin will be more tense and 'stiff' and will not move over his ribs so fluidly. In sickness, particularly, the coat may appear dull and/or 'staring' (standing away from the skin), and the skin tense and stiff. This can also happen if the horse is very uncomfortable such as when left out without protection in inclement weather.

Horses in a good mood or feeling fine normally stand with their polls above their withers, taking notice of their surroundings. If dozing or feeling tired or sleepy, the head will drop somewhat and the tail droop and they may stand with one hind leg bent and resting on the toe. This is a common deportment of dozing horses. They can actually sleep lightly when standing in this same posture, or lying down propped up on their breastbones. They can only experience deep, restorative sleep when lying flat out, which is also when they dream. Horses moved to a new home or a different box on their existing yard may not lie down for some time until they feel safe to do so – a throwback to being aware of predators. If your horse never lies down, he may feel his box is too small to get up again safely or easily, he may be stabled next to or near a horse he dislikes or is afraid of, or he may have physical problems such as arthritis or other pain or stiffness, which a veterinary surgeon could check for you.

What is Your Horse Telling You?

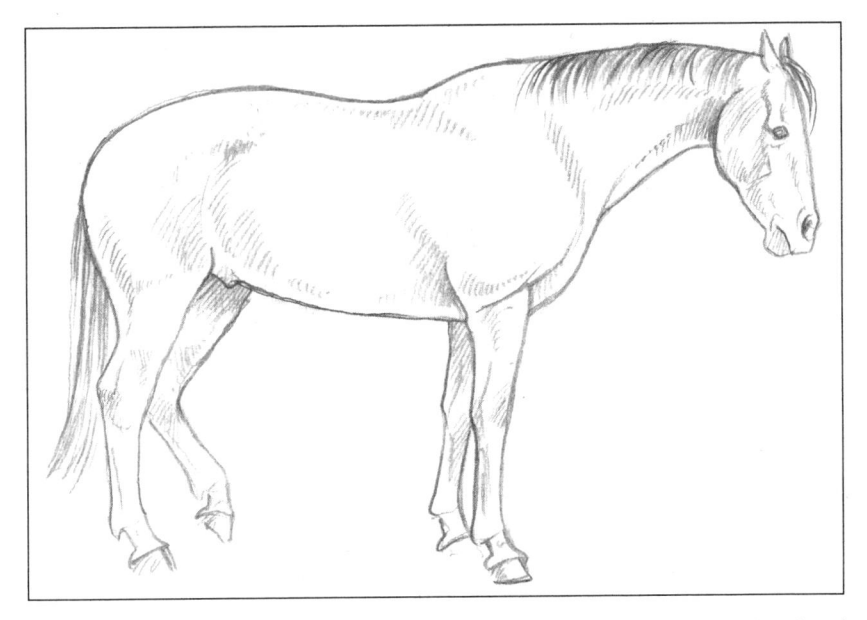

Figure 2.2: A horse who is off colour will withdraw into himself, often head down, not interested in what is going on. His coat may be dull and look rough or 'staring', as it is called.

Horses normally stand with both forefeet more or less next to each other, and fairly still. If a horse moves his weight frequently from one foot to the other, front or back, it indicates pain in one of the feet. A lame leg or painful foot may well be held forward or back from its pair and maybe resting on the toe or, more rarely, heel. If a horse stands with his weight back on to his hind feet, which will be abnormally forward under his body to help his balance, it is almost certainly a sign of laminitis in the fore feet.

The features described are often combined to give a clear picture of how a horse is feeling. So, if you see a ridden horse with his ears hard back, his eyes partially closed or wrinkled into a triangular shape, his nostrils wrinkled up and back, his mouth partly open and his muzzle tense and 'mobile', moving around, he is very unhappy, angry, uncomfortable, maybe experiencing pain from his rider, and distressed because he feels trapped in that situation, and you will know that he has an awful rider!

Figure 2.3: Horses show their feelings plainly. This horse is being ridden harshly and there is no mistaking it. Ears pressed hard back mean pain, distress and anger, his eyes, often with a triangular shape, show anxiety and his open mouth clearly shows great discomfort and probably pain in his mouth from rough or forceful use of the bit.

Frothing at the mouth is **not** a sign of a horse happily champing and accepting his bit but of distress, discomfort, possibly pain, and of being worried about the bit in his mouth. It occurs because the horse, due to an enforced pulled-in head carriage that cramps his throat area, maybe exacerbated by a tight noseband that prevents him opening his mouth, cannot swallow his own saliva, so it froths up in his mouth and spills out around his lips or even down his shoulders and forelegs. For a long time, froth around the mouth has been taken to mean that the horse has a 'soft' mouth and is happily 'playing' with his bit. In happy horses, also with a comfortable noseband (see later in this book), froth does not occur. A horse's mouth should be moist, to enhance sensation and comfort, but with **no** froth. Obvious mouth troubles can also, of course, be due to dental or other mouth disorders.

A horse's general demeanour can tell us a lot about how he is feeling. Pay attention to his normal behaviour and interests and note any deviations from them. If he seems uninterested in life he is either sickening for something, unwell, bored or suffering from a mental/psychological condition indicating some kind of unhappiness. This could be boredom, lack of freedom, frustration maybe due to over-confinement/lack of exercise and freedom, loneliness or grief, lack of other equine company or generally being trapped in an unsuitable lifestyle for him. His general air in such a case will be 'flat' and depressed or he may be performing stereotypical behaviours ('stable vices') to relieve his psychological distress.

Forget the old pronouncement that vices are 'catching'. They aren't. Horses perform them individually when they need to relieve their psychological/mental distress and, as such, the modern advice is to let the horse do so (while also greatly improving his lifestyle) rather than using often rather barbaric means of stopping him. Stereotypies can become a habit in a horse even when his lifestyle is much improved, although they usually lessen somewhat. Incidentally, crib-biters and windsuckers have been found to be more intelligent and possibly sensitive than average.

It is most important that owners and carers familiarise themselves with equine communication. Lack of mutual understanding usually results in us humans getting the idea that a horse is being stubborn, difficult or lazy whereas so very often the reason is that he just doesn't understand what we want and/or is frustrated because he has been telling us something as clearly as he can but we are not taking it in and so are not doing anything about it to help him.

Your horse's moods
Like any living creature, horses have moods. When we decide to ride our horse, maybe in the only time slot we have available

that day, we perhaps don't wonder if the horse is in the mood for working or even going for a leisurely hack. How can we tell?

If you have been in the habit of just being with your horse on a company, friendship basis, as described above, you will reach the point at which you can tell how your horse is feeling. In the next chapter we talk about health parameters, which can certainly affect how a horse is feeling, but here we just need to think about the normal moods a healthy horse will experience.

When you first see your horse on any day, even if you are short of time, take several minutes to talk and listen to him, maybe silently but the result is the same. You will reach the point at which you feel instantly when you see him what mood he is in – bright, pleased to see you, curious as to whether you have anything tasty with you, what mood **you** are in and so on. You will also sense if he is feeling lethargic, fed up, uninterested in anything connected with humans or just not feeling particularly like action stations.

If we just bustle into a horse's box with grooming gear and tack and start preparing him for work straight away, he may well react negatively even if we don't sense it – withdrawing, looking a bit sour or upset, moving away or even nipping to discourage us. When we meet up with a friend, even on the phone, we say 'hello', ask how they are, and spend a few minutes telling each other how we're feeling and so on before getting down to the other business of the call, if any. It's the same with your horse. Horses greet each other in a similar but horsey way, usually sniffing nostrils and, ears pricked, sensing how their friend is feeling. This is natural horse manners as well as human manners, so why not inter-species manners as well? It can be really hurtful to a dog, for instance, who has come to greet you to be ignored, walked past or even told to get out of the way and I believe the same applies to horses; people who treat animals like this don't deserve to associate with them.

During your first few minutes taking in your horse's mood, let him sniff you wherever he wants to, then stroke him gently but confidently and slowly. Touch is an amazing facility for passing information between horse and rider. The right touch can change a horse's mood: it triggers the flow of positive hormones and can invigorate him or calm him, reassure him or encourage him, and you can work this out between you.

The best areas to stroke at first are his shoulder and lower neck and the withers area as this is where horses mutually groom each other with their teeth. He may well want to groom your back in return and my personal view is to let him rather than leave him with a negative feeling of rejection. This real equine communication can do your relationship no end of good, and develop and reinforce your partnership.

Get out of the habit of patting your horse, even gently. To horses, this is the equivalent of a short, sharp shock type of feeling, such as a nip or a kick from another horse, which means in horse language 'go away' in no uncertain terms. It is really poor form for delighted riders to slap and thump their horses at the end of, for instance, a successful jumping round or other victory. They should just stroke their horse and say something like 'good boy' or whatever they use for praise, so that the horse will be appropriately rewarded.

Equitation science has shown us that timing rewards must be fairly instant for the horse to connect the praise or reward with what he has done to deserve it (Chapter 7). Of course, at the end of a round this usually happens too late: it will simply make the horse feel good even though he has nothing to connect it with by the time the rider gets round to it, but it's always right to make your horse feel good, and confirm your friendship.

If you sense, after your enquiries, that your horse is up for a hack and looking forward to working with you, fine, go ahead, but what if he clearly isn't in that mood? You could still tack him up and take him for a short, gentle ride out and see how he feels, but you could also do him a big favour and lead him out for a walk and a graze instead. This closeness will do your relationship just as much good in a different way. Most premises for horses have some spare grassy areas around which could offer your horse a welcome nibble, so put on his head collar, a rug, if necessary, fastened loosely enough at the front to enable him to get his head down in comfort, and just go for a toddle.

If you need to take him off the yard to do this, use a snaffle bridle (for more control) with a movable, jointed bit so that he can actually manoeuvre the grass round it and swallow it. Half-moon mouthpieces often get the grass wrapped round them and make the whole experience frustrating and unpleasant.

What about if your horse is in the opposite mood, full of life, perhaps short of exercise and raring to go? It may even be a good idea, especially on a cold day (when, if he's clipped, he should be wearing an exercise sheet), to start trotting carefully rather than spending your first ten minutes or so in walk to warm up. Steady trotting is fine and will warm up the horse while letting him get the itch out of his heels first. This is also a good opportunity, when you've gauged whether or not he is likely to buck for joy, to give him a long rein and encourage him to stretch his head and neck out and down, which will lift his back and encourage him to use his hind legs well under him without your having to ask any more of him. Change the rein frequently and change often the diagonal on which you rise when on a straight line. Don't plough round and round the outside track but make use of the whole school, or suitable riding areas off your yard. Your horse will soon feel less full of energy and settle to his work or hack.

What if, though, you get the feeling with your initial few minutes' sensing how he is, that he is actually not well, flat, lethargic, weak or just not **right**. Then is the time to study him more closely, perhaps check his temperature, do a skin-pinch test to check the quality of his skin and that he is not dehydrated (check his water is easily accessible, plentiful and **clean**), check the quality of his droppings, urine if possible, his pulse and his breathing, and so on. You could lead him out to see if he's interested in the outdoors, in having some grass and so on, and if he isn't there's almost certainly something wrong. If you are even undecided, I think it's time to call the vet for an initial talk, at least.

Being considerate in this way to your horse is correct and caring horsemanship, or horsemastership, as care and management used to be called. In fact, to not even consider your horse's moods and feelings but carelessly take it for granted that he's fine to work could extend to unintentional cruelty. More than once, I have heard owners say that they pay the bills and do all the work, so the least the horse can do is work for them when required. True. Our horses tell us as clearly as they can how they are: it's one of our main responsibilities to learn to understand, and to act accordingly.

3

Care and Management Really Matter
Feeding, Housing, Bedding, Turnout and General Care

In this chapter:

- ❖ Contentment produces good mental and physical health.
- ❖ The essential basics of The Three F's – Friends, Freedom and Foraging, as defined by the International Society of Equitation Science, in my view probably the most important equestrian organisation today.
- ❖ How to provide what horses really need and suggested compromises, where necessary.
- ❖ Health parameters.

An excellent guide and check for the care and well-being of a healthy, happy horse is to implement the requirements of Friends, Freedom and Foraging – a phrase developed by equitation scientists to put in a nutshell the basic essentials for an animal like a horse. I'm sure you'll know immediately that most horses do not have these three essentials provided in adequate amounts, at least on a daily basis. Part of the problem is the facilities offered, or not offered, on livery yards on which most of our horses live these days.

Wherever your horse calls home, those three things truly can make it into a real home with some ingenuity, thought and compassion on our part. There are other aspects of good management, of course, but we'll take those elements one by one first of all.

Friends

We can be in no doubt that horses are herd animals. They evolved to be together in fairly small groups, the number in a feral family herd usually being at most twelve or so and often fewer than that. There is one main, serving stallion who is a lodger, not the herd boss, and maybe younger colts, probably his sons but maybe the sons of a previous stallion. These may or may not mate the herd's mares, perhaps when the stallion isn't looking.

Young males may be ousted by the stallion from the herd when they reach puberty but young females tend to stay with the family and are very close to their dams. Groups of single males are known as bachelor bands and may live together for years, but often a stallion will hang around other herds and try to take mares to form a herd of his own. This can be difficult because mares and daughters are close, and the older mares, maybe one in particular, are quite autocratic, but it does happen and, so, inbreeding is reduced or prevented.

It is obvious at once that this natural horse life is nothing like the life we expect horses in domesticity to adapt to. However, it is possible to create it in a domestic setting: I was very interested, some decades ago, to see a similar experiment at Ireland's National Stud, obviously with Thoroughbreds, and it worked well, with happy, calm, healthy and fertile horses. The mares and stallion lived out and mated at will and at liberty, providing an interesting and rare study opportunity for the stud's students. The stallion had seemed infertile when mated in a conventional domestic manner but every one of his mares in the experiment conceived!

Figure 3.1: Horses cement their friendships by 'mutual grooming'. They rub each other, sometimes quite hard, with their front teeth, usually in the neck, withers, shoulder and back area, mainly near the spine. Here, one horse's hindquarters are also receiving welcome attention.

The only suggestion of a natural life in a domestic stable yard, livery or otherwise, is when horses are turned out together, and even then they often don't get to choose their own 'herd' mates. If we use our common horse sense, we only turn out horses who get on with each other, especially if they are shod because skirmishes can easily result in quite serious injuries. In any equine scenario, accidents can happen, but I believe that this is a risk we must bear for our horses' sakes. We cannot, if we care about their mental contentment and happiness (which affects their physical health), avoid taking **some** risk with their physical safety. After all, we put it at risk every time we ride them.

Another aspect of domestic turnout nowadays is often to separate mares and geldings. Again, not only is this an unnatural situation but also it is unnecessary. Mares and geldings can form strong friendships and enmities with each other just like horses of the same sex and it is unkind, and I think bad management, to separate them and deny them the chance to enjoy and nurture their friendship in a fairly free situation. Remember, happiness equals good health! It also won't reduce arguments between horses. The important thing is to turn out **compatible, friendly** horses together.

This single-sex turnout seems to have really developed over the past couple of decades here in the UK, partly to reduce accidents and partly to prevent horses over-eating grass. It might slightly reduce accidents (I don't find that it does).

What I call 'the postage stamp system' of turnout (tiny patches of land taped off with electric fencing) may be better than being stabled all the time but cannot make for happy horses, simply increasing their frustration in a 'so near yet so far' way – they can see their friends yet cannot socialise naturally with them over an electric fence. A second source of frustration for them is that such overgrazed land is unhealthy, sour and hard to access, even for horses, who have the ability to graze 'closely' like sheep, because it never gets a chance to reach a normal height for grazing. A good horse-care policy allows horses to form normal friendships as naturally as possible.

Wherever you keep your horse or horses, I hope you will be able to arrange matters so that they are out as much as is reasonably possible and allowed to make friends in a stable group, so experiencing something adequately approaching a natural lifestyle for a good part of their day. When turnout is impossible, hopefully for short periods, grazing friends out in hand together, hacking together and being stabled next to each other with contact facilities are all ways of giving them one of the above three basic essentials which are so often lacking in domestic life.

Freedom

Liberty for free, active and energetic movement and the psychological advantages of feeling free should be regarded as a priority for all horses under normal conditions. I feel that its value and necessity is very often greatly under-estimated and regarded as a treat rather than essential to a happy, healthy life. Many people believe that an hour's ridden exercise or work every day is enough to keep a horse healthily exercised and mentally satisfied, but it really isn't. Unfortunately, many establishments, private and commercial, do not offer anything like sufficient facilities for enough daily freedom for horses, even when they are available.

It is understandable that land can become susceptible to lasting damage if used by horses when very wet, so some periods will arise when it is out of use. Some don't have enough, or even any, turnout land. Most, though, such as urban yards, have exercise facilities in the form of indoor and/or outdoor schools, horse-walkers, gallops or hacking circuits and can use the first two for giving horses a freedom of sorts in pairs or small groups. Unfortunately, even with such facilities they are often not used for that important purpose, either because they are constantly in use or because it is claimed that no one has time to pick up the droppings (which occur with ridden horses, anyway) or because horses cavorting around will disturb the expensive surface (as can ordinary work and, particularly, jumping).

It is easy to disregard the fact that all equestrian establishments exist because of the horses, not solely for our purposes with them. It is also easy to overlook another fact – that horses given ample freedom, preferably daily, are actually easier to handle, train, ride and look after. They are more settled mentally, regularly and naturally exercised physically which is part of good care and are altogether even more rewarding to be around because they are happy.

Care and Management Really Matter

Figure 3.2: These horses are enjoying two of the three basic essentials for horse happiness and well-being – friends and freedom in togetherness. The third is foraging or searching for food. It is sad that so many horses are denied all three of these crucial features.

Horses, like us, become acclimatised to weather and seasonal conditions and not all like being out twenty-four hours a day, particularly if there is insufficient shelter. A man-made shelter is best because insects gather under trees and near shrubbery in warmer seasons but seem to dislike entering artificial shelters such as field shelters or barns converted for horse use. They can be a source of real torture to horses, as can inescapable strong sunshine and excessive heat. Horses often dislike the opposite conditions – cold, especially, wet and windy weather, and mud. They naturally stand with their tails to the wind so are more comfortable with tails left full at the top, which also protects a sensitive area in summer. Even without a decent shelter, some time, in addition to work or exercise, should be regarded as a must on most days – but what if it really cannot be arranged? Here are some compromises.

Leading out in hand has already been mentioned. Time-consuming though this may be, it does have its rewards. Firstly and most importantly, horses enjoy it. Secondly, they are mentally and physically engaged in something which, left to nature, they would be doing for about sixteen hours a day – grazing and browsing – so are happy, calm and fulfilled. The grass is their natural food and you will surely find that being together and creating pleasure for your horse mutually enhances your relationship.

If you can't be present but can find someone you can trust, whether or not you pay them or do something for them in return, you can have your horse exercised (ridden or led) for longer than usual, or in two spells to break up the long drag of being stabled and, let's face it, confined unnaturally for about twenty-two hours out of the twenty-four. Be careful of lungeing because most people do it wrongly – too fast and on too-small circles, both of which are damaging to your horse. Years ago, I was lucky enough to keep a horse at a yard where there was someone good at long-reining, and when adequate turnout was not possible, he used to long-rein my mare around the village in the afternoon, in addition to my morning ride, to everyone's enjoyment as she was very sociable and picked up lots of treats on her travels. She seemed to find it more like 'time off', to be walking ahead, no rider, in charge, and deciding where and when she would stop if she saw someone known for carrying titbits. As a former racehorse, and with her 'long-reiner' a former racing head lad, theirs was the ideal combination.

It may be possible to rent some temporary grazing locally and let your horse (with a friend) be taken there and back preferably daily. Whatever you can arrange will be better than inadequate or no freedom at all. Activity and freedom are so very important to horses; perhaps we need to think more about how we can provide them when facilities are wanting.

Foraging

Foraging – exploring, finding, sorting out, choosing, chomping and relishing the results – is what horses naturally do most of but, it seems to me, generally do much too little of in domestic life for lack of opportunity. I think this is mainly because most of us do not fully realise how very important it is to horses' physical and mental health. In some quarters of the horse world, there is a belief that bulky, roughage foods like hay, haylage and grass should be restricted, not only when horses are working athletically but as a normal, daily principle. It is believed that concentrates are more nutritious and, so, are better for the horses, that bulky foods are second-rate and more like 'padding out' the diet, with little nutritious value.

Nothing could be further from the truth. Although horses living a natural life with many miles to roam over only ever found what we call concentrates – the seeds of plants – in late summer and autumn when the plants had gone to seed, for the rest of the year grass and other plants, including leaves from trees, were all they had, and usually plenty of them, yet they travelled regularly about 40 kilometres or 25 miles a day at active paces with no ill effects like strenuous overwork. How many domestic horses or ponies do that?

It's hard to argue with nature when it comes to evolution and survival, even though feral horses do not live as long as domestic ones usually are allowed to. The seeds eaten in autumn and early winter helped to top up the horses' body condition in preparation for winter because winter forage is of low nutritional value and not very palatable. The old description of spring grass – Dr Green – was very apt because at the end of winter young, nutritious grass was just what horses needed to prepare them for the demanding breeding season.

It is also perhaps not known that feral-living equines are much fitter than most domestic horses. They are almost constantly on the move at gentle gaits like walk and trot, unlike mainly stabled horses, and canter about when they want to if, for example, playing, and sometimes gallop in fun but also if they experience danger such as a predator. Being together all the time, they also use muscles playing and interacting with herd mates – and we all know how rough and energetic horse play can be.

The horse's digestive system is geared to needing, and being able to cope with, forage-type feed as its basis. If a horse goes for more than four hours without food, its digestive organisms that break down and digest the food start to die off. They are then less numerous when food finally does arrive and this can result in basic indigestion but also colic which, as we all know, is extremely painful. Colic can be followed by laminitis due to the toxins produced, and both conditions can be fatal.

Owners who know this take pains to find forage feeds which their conscientious growers and/or merchants have sent to be analysed, so that their levels of energy, protein and other nutrients are known. This means that horses and ponies on fairly undemanding work schedules or who easily put on too much weight – at the risk of laminitis – can be given lower-energy forage feeds.

If you buy forage that has not been analysed, you can 'dilute' it by giving part forage, part straw. Oat and barley straw are better for feeding than wheat straw, although that can be better than nothing. Small ponies can be at risk of suffering an intestinal blockage when feeding high-fibre feeds like straw, so it is always a good plan to consult an equine nutritionist, either an independent one or one at the firm whose feeds you use, to discuss this.

Bagged forage feeds today are generally excellent and are carefully formulated for different nutritional levels and uses but are not cheap. Again, a discussion with a nutritionist should help you to come up with a suitable diet for your horse at an acceptable price.

If you use really good quality hay and haylage, or bagged forage, your horse may very well not need additional concentrates. We have been brought up for a couple of generations to believe that they are necessary, but today we also have far more cases of laminitis than in the past and far too many overweight, indeed obese, animals than we ever saw in the past, and I've been around horses all my fairly long life.

To encourage you to regard your horse's fibrous, bulky, forage as being the most important item in his diet, unless he is working very hard, here is something that might make you consider another way. Years ago, I used to write for a professional magazine in the horse world called *Stable Management.* Another of its authors, whose name I genuinely forget but who was a very experienced, all-round horseman a good deal older than me, wrote an article about feeding hard-working horses, mainly hunters doing four or five hard days a fortnight, during the war years when oats were reserved for human consumption. He, too, felt that too much emphasis was starting to be placed, in what would be the 1960s and 1970s, on concentrate feeds and explained how hunters and other hard-working horses were fed mainly on high quality seed hay and more or less as much as they wanted. They also had bran, linseed and various root feeds such as carrots, of course, but also turnips, fodder beets and others. Their main nutrition, however, came from their hay. They worked just as well as before their dietary 'restriction', maintained their weight, fitness and well-being and seemed, in fact, healthier and happier on this more natural diet. Worth considering, I think.

If your horse does not work particularly hard and/or has a weight problem, it is even more important to be **very** careful to feed enough to prevent hunger but keep the energy content of his feeds low. Again, I recommend that you talk to a qualified equine nutritionist regarding a suitable energy level for your horse. All good feed companies offer free helplines. The nutritionist will note your horse's or pony's type, age, work, lifestyle, health history, current diet including grazing, personality and so on and give you reliable information on what would give you the best results while taking care of his digestive comfort, health and ability to work, or not work.

We all know that dietary changes should be made gradually, over about a month, to allow the digestive micro-organisms to adapt their populations to cope with the differences. This applies to hay and haylage as well as manger feeds. This also gives the horse chance to adapt to different tastes and will give you an idea of whether the new feed is going to be acceptable to your horse.

My old mare, mentioned above, was a **very** finicky feeder. She always left a spoonful of feed at the bottom of her manger – no idea why – and at first I had to change her feed gradually all the time to get her to eat, until I hit on one she loved, and she stuck to it for the rest of her life. She was one of those (an old Thoroughbred) who could not have managed on only hay, except possibly when on summer grass, so even then she had small manger feeds. She looked forward to them, having been kept that way all her long life before I bought her, so I kept to that regime. It's well worth really going out of your way to suit your horse. They are our prisoners, after all, and depend on us for everything. The reward you get from seeing a horse bloom under your care is truly priceless.

Forage and foraging are so very important to horses for both entertainment and nutritional value that it is worth giving them much higher status than we may have done so far. Many stereotypies ('stable vices') occur due to stress, it's true, and boredom is a big part of the stress experienced by stabled horses and ponies, especially those not given enough forage. Ample, suitable forage goes a very long way to relieving or eliminating this stress, poor health and unhappiness.

Water
Although it can be difficult to get us humans to drink enough plain water, it really is a crucially important part of a horse's diet

and they normally drink very freely when their water is easily accessible, clean and fresh. An average riding horse can drink roughly 23 to 45 litres/5 to 10 gallons a day, depending on the weather and his work.

Free-living horses naturally drink from ground level, of course, but stabled horses often have automatic drinkers fitted to save their attendants work. This is fine, except that the drinkers are usually, I find, fitted much too high for the horses to drink comfortably, so they end up not drinking nearly enough. I remember visiting a yard of mainly ponies who, very obviously, could not drink at all comfortably from the drinkers, which were at a height meant for horses – and too high for them, too. The owner commented that the ponies often got colic, and some of the horses as well. I tactfully pointed out that the drinkers were much too high, even though they were at the height recommended by the makers. He said he could not afford to have them replaced, understandably, so reverted to buckets for the ponies and smaller horses.

(To digress slightly, I once visited a mounted police horse yard for the purpose of writing about them, and the stable manager commented that the horses rarely finished their 'manger' feeds. The stables had been, very expensively, designed by a respected firm of architects who had done their research and told the police that horses should eat from ground level. This was accepted, so the architects fitted each stable with containers set down into the floor of the stables, with their top edges **level with the floor** and, therefore, the food below ground level. You can see where this is leading. The resulting manger-sized 'wells' being so low, the horses could not reach the food at all easily, especially as the level dropped, despite trying various contortions such as bending one knee at a time, or even two. One horse, apparently, even knelt on both knees – very unpleasant for a horse – to reach his food and even then his grooms did not realise why. Much of the food was left, of course, tantalising the horses between meals – and the attendants wondered why they seemed stressed and were weaving and crib-biting.

(Strangely, the architects did not follow what they had discovered for the hay and water. Hay was fed in head-level racks or conventional hay nets and the drinkers at elbow level. I did point out the problem with the feed containers but whether anything was done about it I don't know.)

Horses should, indeed, eat and drink mainly with their polls lower than their withers, as described earlier, so that their natural eating and drinking mechanism can work properly. If horses pull hay from a high rack or net, or pull down leaves from trees, you'll see that they usually drop their heads to a comfortable height so that they can chew and swallow properly.

To get back to water, natural sources such as streams running through a field, or ponds, are often much favoured by horses but should be checked very regularly for purity and safety by sending a sample to an appropriate laboratory (ask your vet).

Water in field troughs fed by a domestic supply pipe should be fine, but can become polluted by dead birds or animals that have drowned in it and are decomposing. Such troughs should really be scrubbed out (no soap!) fairly often to help with hygiene – and any corpses removed as soon as possible.

Where water is provided in buckets in stables, it is a good plan to provide two in different corners, the same ones all the time, so that if the horse does a dropping in one the other will be available. The water should be changed several times a day, not topped up. In fields, water can be provided by hosepipe to plastic tubs fixed to the fence (not in a corner). These can be moved along to prevent poaching in wet weather, which is an advantage.

Take care to note how much, and how, your horse is drinking. This is easier with buckets on the ground as you can see how much he is taking. Drinking too little or too much can be due to dental, mouth or throat problems or to other illness.

Housing

I have called this section 'Housing' because there are several ways of providing a horse with indoor living facilities other than conventional stabling. Keeping a horse at livery may restrict your options unless you can find a forward-thinking, horse-loving yard owner willing to adapt facilities.

Conventional stables are often three blank, roof-high walls with the only opening the top door of the stable, maybe with a window next to it. In these, ventilation is often poor, they can be dark and certainly claustrophobic for an animal like a horse. They have no facility for horses to communicate with neighbours and are merely better than keeping a horse (depending on the horse) out all the time in all weathers. They certainly do not promote equine mental health if the horses are rarely allowed out. Horse-to-horse, tactile contact is extremely important to horses and it is impossible in such stables.

Stale air also rises, not always finding its way out of the door or window, but pooling at the top of the often too-low stable. (Stables should be high enough to prevent a rearing horse banging his head on the roof. The size of the box should be a minimum of 12 feet x 12 feet/3.65 metres square for a horse of about 15 hands high/152.4 cm.) Smells from bedding, especially if not fully mucked out every day, can quickly accumulate in such a confined airspace. Ammonia in the air is a frequent result of dirty bedding. It is corrosive and irritating and can burn the nose, throat, eyes and respiratory tract, significantly injuring and damaging the tissues, maybe even resulting in respiratory distress or failure.

Loose boxes (US stalls) of conventional design can be greatly improved by having ridge-roof ventilators installed so that the warm, rising air actually escapes and keeps the stable air fresher. Boxes with more than one outlook are a boon to horses. They like a view from not only the front of their stables but the sides and/or back as well. You can have outlets fitted with safety plastic doors that can be opened or closed depending on the prevailing weather direction, but the horses can still see through them when they are closed. I have found horses really love these.

Chat holes have already been mentioned and are much appreciated. Dividing walls that are not solid all the way along (only perhaps at the back where the horses eat) are a major improvement and are usually of vertical railings at the front parts of the walls. The bars should be too narrow to permit a hoof through them but horses can touch and communicate well. The bars are desirable to prevent the possibility of a horse trying to jump over the lower part of the partition and maybe getting stuck.

Where possible, it is a wonderful facility to have a small, fenced yard at the front, side or back of the box so that the horse can come in and out and be with his neighbours as he wishes but still be contained. I have seen this arrangement with serving stallions, stabled away from the mares in the evenings (they were turned out with their own herds during the day) and they were much appreciated and I was told there was never any trouble.

Field shelters of various kinds can be arranged, and movable ones on skids can be towed to a new site to prevent poaching of the ground. An ideal arrangement is a large shed or small barn opening on to the field or paddock, which is really welcomed by horses out a good deal. It may not be necessary to bed it down, but it should be skipped out daily and can be supplied with hay and possibly water.

If large enough indoor spaces are available, there is nothing wrong with two ponies or horses sharing one large box. Two small stables could be made into one, or some other building could be converted with a little imagination.

Really, there are no limits to our imaginations. Some simple changes could make all the difference to your horses' lives and happiness.

Figure 3.3: Many horses don't mind being in their stables for limited periods, but most boxes are too small. This is a good-sized box, and would actually stand having two friendly horses in it together for company. The hay/haylage tubs in different corners can hold different types of forage to give the horse variety, and there is **no** restrictive, claustrophobic weaving grille above the door, a welcome omission. If a horse wants to weave, he will weave inside the box, anyway.

Bedding

There is no doubt that horses love fresh, deep, dry bedding to roll in and lie on. Here in the UK the main bedding materials are wood shavings and wheat straw. The worldwide economy has hit the horse world like everything else and materials that were once cheap are now a financial consideration for everyone. The fact remains, though, that horses kept in stables need bedding and they like it to be clean, dry, fairly deep and without an objectionable smell.

Mucking out is a twice-daily chore that is an **important** task to promote the horse's well-being. It is a time-consuming, labour intensive job and bedding is no longer cheap – all the more reason to turn our horses out to save on these aspects. If horses are in all night the main muck-out will be in the **morning after turning out**, and perhaps vice versa in summer. Although security is a consideration, in summer most horses are **happier out at night** and in during the day away from heat and insects. For horses in much of their time, a main muck-out in the morning is needed with regular skipping out (removing just the droppings) during the day, topping up the bedding as needed.

How deep is just right? Certainly a scattering of a couple of inches is no good. It does not encourage horses to lie and rest and thin beds absorb the urine and become tainted by droppings quicker and more thoroughly than a good thick bed of about 15 cm/6 inches or a bit more. Shavings pack down more than straw, but all in all it shouldn't be too easy to reach the floor below.

The object of mucking and skipping out, of course, is to keep a fairly clean, **dry** bed for your horse, so in a main muck-out all wet and very damp bedding needs to come out along with all droppings. Although horses don't mind lying down on wet grass, they dislike lying in their own urine although they may not have a choice, and all the moisture in a horse's bed is urine. It's fine to leave a thin layer of just-damp bedding on the floor itself and covering it with dry bedding.

Banks round the sides of a loose box/stall, which will be dry, can be brought down and spread evenly, then fresh bedding spread on top and also used to make new banks. I don't like the practice of leaving banks in place long-term because urine seeps around under the bedding and can be soaked up into the banks, creating an unhealthy, mouldy and diseased environment. I prefer to take banks down completely every day because the bedding will be clean and can be used on the bed, new banks being stacked up, if you wish, with fresh bedding. I am also not convinced, either, that banks stop horses becoming cast, although that is the general reason for having them.

Thin day beds are useless, in my view, for reasons given above. Also, if horses have been out all night they will want to lie down and rest in comfort, which they can't experience on a thin bed.

Whatever your choice, remember the watchwords are: 'clean', 'dry' and 'plentiful'.

'Paddock paradises'

Any feature on improving horses' living conditions must include the current, increasing trend to create 'paddock paradises' which allow horses freedom, promote exercise, allow herd-type company and generally make life easier for everyone, equine and human.

Not simply turning out horses into a field or paddock more than usual, paddock paradises are normally, a series of tracks created between paddocks, with water and shelter facilities included. The paddocks have individual gates which can be opened to allow the horses on to possibly one paddock at a time, where there are often no facilities but grazing. Shelter, water and supplementary hay, according to requirements, are sited around the site, causing horses to walk to them when they need them. There may be only one water point, which horses walk to several times a day, and there can be covered areas or areas for shelter along the track, barns or whatever can be arranged, and hay provided in one or two places, but usually not in the paddocks.

This is a very loose description of the system, which can vary considerably, but the upshot of it is that horses have company, grazing, water, shelter and, when required, hay. They have to keep on the move to access each different facility, which encourages mobility, basic fitness, occupation, application and more herd-like behaviour.

Horses on these systems are bright and interested in life, healthy, content and fitter than those conventionally stabled and turned out. Like horses mostly living out, they can be caught up and ridden and turned out again with no problem. They quickly learn the ins and outs of their set-up, including when access to a paddock changes, although they might need showing which gate is opened when a new paddock is brought into use. They can be partly stabled, if desired, although it is best for two at once to be taken from the herd to avoid a single one becoming very fretful.

Health parameters

Checking on a horse's daily condition and demeanour should be second nature, but it is also necessary to keep a check on specific health matters, say on a weekly basis or more frequently if it is suspected something is not right.

The following are general guidelines that an owner can check:

- General appearance and behaviour
- Body condition or weight
- Temperature, pulse and respiration (TPR)
- Eating habits
- Elimination habits (urine and faeces/droppings)
- Action and testing for lameness

General appearance and behaviour

We have already mentioned tuning in to a horse to gauge how he is feeling and how he seems whether he is healthy or not. Getting to know his normal way of being, moods and behaviour is a good baseline to check him against, particularly if he is not well, so you can gauge his recovery. A bright, interested appearance, eating well, lying down freely, having no difficulty in getting up, being pleased to see humans or at least showing some level of interest – these are all things that can change when a horse is off colour.

Body condition or weight

We rightly hear a lot, these days, about many horses, particularly cobs and ponies, being unhealthily overweight. Overweight and obesity have just the same risk of triggering other, serious health conditions as they have in humans or any other animal.

It is good to get a weigh tape and check your horse weekly when you do your general check mentioned above, but an excellent and very simple way of gauging his weight is simply that you should be able to feel his ribs **easily** but not see them, unless he is turning away from you. If you can actually see his ribs when he is just standing still or moving straight ahead, he is probably too thin. Even very fit horses should be reasonably covered. But if you have to push a bit and feel around for his ribs, he is probably slightly overweight, or more.

These two points indicate that a change in diet is needed, and anything markedly above or below the simple standard given above could beneficially be discussed with a nutritionist or vet to effect a gradual correction in the horse's condition. Starving or minimalist diets are not the answer for fat horses or ponies unless the situation is urgent and on a vet's advice: neither is rapidly and considerably increasing the amount or nutritional content of a feed to boost a thin animal. Changes should, as mentioned, generally be made gradually so that the body can adapt and cope.

Temperature, pulse and respiration

These three pointers, known as a horse's 'vital signs', are an excellent guide to general health or the seriousness and progress of a disorder. Taking them on a weekly basis with your general check gets both horse and carer used to the process and makes any irregularity quickly spotted.

Temperature: The normal temperature of an average horse is about 38 °C or 100.4 °F. To take it you will need a thermometer either digital or 'traditional' glass-and-mercury type. The former are more accurate than they used to be and are simply placed on the thin skin at the side of the dock. The older type is very accurate and is inserted into the horse's rectum.

To do this, shake the mercury well down until it is well below the normal rate, moisten the bulb with either spit or Vaseline jelly and, standing behind and to the left of your horse (if right-handed), bring the dock sideways towards you with the four fingers of your left hand and, with a swivelling, side-to-side motion of the thermometer, insert the bulb straight into the anus, pushing it well in but keeping a secure hold on it; don't let go. Press the bulb gently against the side of the rectum and leave it in for the time stated on it. Pull it out, wipe it quickly on the tail hair and read the temperature. Sterilise the thermometer before putting it away.

The temperature can vary with the weather and, particularly, with fast work. Take it while your horse is relaxed and if it is approaching two degrees above or below the normal weekly rate, ring your vet for a discussion. Look for other signs of possible ill-health, as mentioned.

Pulse: The normal pulse rate is about 32 to 42 beats per minute (bpm), smaller animals having a faster pulse than larger ones. There is a knack to taking the pulse. Personally, I can never find the ones in the fetlock. The pulse can be felt wherever an artery crosses over a bone (they say!). Likely areas are under and inside the round jawbone, above the outer corner of the eye, inside the elbow, at the side of or under the dock about a third of the way down, and on the arteries passing over the inside and outside of the fetlock joints.

You need to feel about a bit and give time for the pulse to occur. Use the tips of your four fingers close together and leave them in place for several seconds. Use a watch that indicates seconds, count the beats for half a minute and double it to give you the beats per minute. Obviously, your horse or pony should not have worked or been upset recently: he needs to be quiet and calm. Again, if there is a significant difference from his normal weekly rate, ring your vet.

Respiration: The normal rate for an average horse is eight to sixteen breaths per minute, maybe more in warm weather and certainly if the horse has recently been moving about or has been particularly alert. It is quite hard to spot a resting horse breathing, but if you approach him and start stroking him, he will wake up a bit and his breathing will become slightly more noticeable. If you stand behind him and a little to one side, watch his opposite flank and you will see it rise and fall with his breathing so you can count each rise and fall as one breath. You can feel his breath with your hand or hold a mirror up to his nostril to see it misting up, but these two methods often intrigue the horse and he will sniff your hand or the mirror, so they are not so reliable as watching the flank.

These vital signs are a great help in assessing your horse's health and condition, so get to know your horse's norms under identical conditions weekly, and any time he seems unwell.

Your back-up
Every conscientious horse-owner needs an up-to-date veterinary book, and it's a good idea to read it when you get it even if there appears nothing wrong with your horse. Veterinary topics go out of date very quickly and any book more than five years old should, I believe, be replaced by a newer one. Look at the front page of small print, giving disclaimers, publisher and so on, where you will find the date the book was first published, to let you know how old yours is. The information inside it will be at least a year older due to the lengthy process of actually publishing a book. Your vet should be able to recommend a suitable book.

Eating habits
The phrase 'eating like a horse' was not coined for nothing. We know already that horses need to eat for about sixteen hours a day and their appetite is a very useful guide to their state of health and well-being. Like any other animal, including humans, horses may have individual eating habits, preferences, times for eating

and so on, and the more you familiarise yourself with these the better idea you will have of how he is on a daily basis.

If your horse unusually leaves his feed he could just not like what you have given him if you are making a change, or he could be sickening for something, just as we and other animals can go off their feed. Horses sometimes do this after hard work, or don't eat at a time when they are normally resting or, of course, if their teeth are making eating painful or difficult. Horses that have been ridden harshly and have a bit injury may naturally not eat so enthusiastically, if at all. A sore throat is as uncomfortable for them as for us and will affect eating habits. Emotions also affect appetite and horses recently deprived of their friends, changing homes, going away to a competition or having to stay at a veterinary hospital, for example, may stop eating for a while or eat little.

Horses' teeth are tremendous crushing tools capable of dealing with tough, fibrous food if necessary, but they do not wear evenly on their opposite numbers. The top teeth are set very slightly wider than the lower ones, so, with wear, the outsides of the upper back teeth which do the grinding, and the insides of the lower ones become sharp. A common cause of deterioration and death in feral horses that are not killed by predators is these sharp edges becoming so long that the horse can sometimes not even close his mouth, let alone eat, and starves to death. Also, depending on the usual head position when eating, hooks can form on the very backs and fronts of the back teeth (molars and pre-molars), and at other sites, which can make eating uncomfortable. A good, qualified horse dental technician or vet can deal with these and increase the horse's comfort and processing of his food. Young and old horses should have their teeth checked and maybe treated every six to twelve months.

Horses' teeth erupt (rather than actually grow) all their lives until only the softer roots remain, at which point they need a softer, nutritious diet; they usually cannot manage to eat much fibrous food, and need careful management and veterinary supervision.

Elimination habits (urine and faeces/droppings)

As vegetarians eating great amounts of fibrous, vegetable matter, horses will do around eight piles of droppings every day. They are a very good guide to general health so get to know what is normal for your horse. Horses mainly stabled on 'stable' food will have brownish droppings with lots of little fibrous pieces in them and just break on hitting the ground whereas those on mainly grass have softer, green droppings.

Urine is usually yellow in colour and can be clear or slightly cloudy. It has a familiar but not particularly unpleasant smell.

Getting to know your horse's normal elimination habits is good management. An unusual colour of either droppings or urine, especially if you see blood or a darker, reddish or purple colour can indicate internal bleeding. If the horse stands unusually while staling or doing a dropping this is a sign of discomfort. If there is a change in consistency or amount of droppings such as diarrhoea or constipation, there is a problem. If a horse tries unsuccessfully to urinate there could be a urinary tract infection and the horse will be in considerable discomfort. A bad smell of either droppings or urine also indicates trouble. Don't delay to ring your vet at least for a discussion but probably for a visit.

Action and testing for lameness

Do make yourself familiar with your horse's normal action in all gaits (see Chapter 5). Not all horses move straight but most manage to get through life without any real problems or even hitting their own legs. Some horses have 'flat' actions and some are naturally springy, some are economical in their action and others are more 'lifted', 'extravagant' or showy. We have our preferences as to action but straightness first is a good plan if you can get it. This means that the hind legs follow exactly the path through the air of the front ones, when the horse is moving in a straight line.

Any deviation, at least in theory, means that the horse is not loading his limbs evenly and that they are more at risk of excess stress and, therefore, lameness. This is, indeed, true, but I would say that there are more crooked movers, if only slightly so, than dead straight ones, and they seem to stay sound, although they might not do so under the demands of hard work.

A horse's feet, like ours, are most instrumental in creating a horse's movement and action: any pain or discomfort here will change a horse's action and the discomfort, pain even, can travel all the way up to his back because he will be holding himself differently to avoid it. This will cause unnatural muscle use in his back and possibly elsewhere in his body and, again, create pain there as well. Any of us who has experienced uncomfortable feet or shoes, a back, leg or foot injury, knows that we cannot walk normally. Our weight distribution is foreign to us, recruiting different muscles from usual in a way different from how they were meant to work. This stresses them, perhaps causing more pain – and exhaustion from the effort of just trying to move. It is just the same for our horses. Not only that: such struggling horses often hit themselves or even stagger and fall and, so, are dangerous to ride if their owners/riders have not recognised what is happening.

Check your horse's action regularly, in your weekly check, but make a habit of keeping an eye on it, and on all the other aspects we have discussed in this chapter, and get professional help from vet or farrier, for your horse's sake. This might be unpopular, but I beg you not to make social media your first port in a storm. You could easily be badly led astray and it will be your horse and your bank balance that will suffer.

Testing for lameness

Another part of our weekly check, this is a basic skill that can spot things going wrong very early if you know what to look for. Early lameness, not yet spotted, will show up on a good check. It doesn't take long and sharpens your eye for your horse's comfort.

Have him in a head collar and lead rope and ask a sensible friend to trot him up on a smooth, hard surface, free of stones, pebbles and grit. Have him trotted away from and towards you. Your handler should trot him away in a straight line on a **loose** rope so he can move naturally and back towards you the same way. Even very slight lameness shows up in trot.

To check the hind legs: when he is trotting away from you, the hock and fetlock of the sound leg will drop the most because that leg is taking more weight. The lame leg hock will stay higher than its pair and the fetlock will drop less because the horse is 'saving' it, putting more weight on to the other hind leg. If you watch the horse from the side, particularly on a bend, you will see the lame leg takes a shorter stride than its pair.

To check the forelegs: watch his head as he is trotting towards you. When the sound leg hits the ground, his head will drop more than when the lame leg does so. This is because he is putting more weight over on to the sound leg and saving the lame one. When he lands the lame leg, his head will be higher to try to take weight off it. On a bend, the lame leg always takes a shorter stride than the sound one.

Feel the lame leg with your bare hands and compare its temperature to the sound one. Any area of heat is where the problem is, from the hoof to the elbow, although most lameness occurs from the knee or hock downwards. Warm feet indicate possible laminitis. Laminitis demands immediate veterinary attention but for slight lameness in other areas you can give the horse 24-hours' box rest, that is, in his box with no riding or turnout. If he is still lame after that time, ring your vet.

An entertaining farrier

Another old saying – 'no foot, no horse' – is so very true. A good farrier is worth his weight in gold. Years ago, it was taken for granted that farriers were (then) quirky and difficult to deal with. An excellent but, yes, quirky one I had explained this by saying that they were all a bit mad: you had to be to spend half your life bent double under the back end of a horse and get your head **** on daily! He had a point. I had an excellent working relationship with him and learnt how to handle him.

One morning he turned up to shoe my horse still drunk from the night before. He controlled his stagger quite well as he wound his way to her box and gave me a sheepish smile. Before he could say a word, I smiled reassuringly at him because I knew he could be struck off for this. I just asked him to do a remove and come back another day to shoe her because I didn't want him nailing on in that state. He thanked me profusely for not reporting him. For a very short time, he had an apprentice who was a pain in the neck and had no right to be around horses. This bolshy, young lad hit my horse with a rasp for putting her foot in the box containing the nails etc. that he had left too close to her. I grabbed the rasp off him, gave him a very strong earful and told him most impolitely to go away. I also told the farrier to keep him well away from me and my mare in future. He sacked him the week after.

4

Tack, Clothing and Protective Items
There is More to it than you Think

In this chapter:

- ❖ Your tack is your link to your horse.
- ❖ Putting his comfort first.
- ❖ The necessity for a properly fitted saddle, girth, bit and bridle for both of you.
- ❖ Bridles and bits to help you both, not torture your horse.
- ❖ The trouble with boots.
- ❖ Not all rugs are horse-friendly.

I firmly believe that horses suffer more from ill-fitting, wrongly adjusted and unsuitable tack than is generally realised. Once the tack is on, the horse can do nothing about it, if it is uncomfortable or painful, other than try to move in a way that lessens the discomfort and pain, which might indicate to his rider that he is being difficult or unwilling. If things are **really** uncomfortable or painful, a horse might play up and be reprimanded for it when it isn't his fault, but the rider may not understand what the problem is, particularly if he or she has fitted it according to the advice of a teacher or other experienced person.

So often, it is clear that a horse is battling a harsh bit contact, an excruciatingly tight bridle and a saddle, and an unavoidable girth that have been fitted too far forward. This very common scenario has several adverse effects on the horse. If he also has a less-than-sympathetic and maybe unskilled rider on his back as well, his life in the immediate future is going to be, shall we say 'difficult', to put it mildly.

Your tack is your link with your horse, meant to make life easier for both of you and, if it is well-fitted and adjusted to accommodate the horse's make and shape, it will be one less problem for him to cope with and, ideally, a help towards a good, painless performance, whether you are out for a hack or competing on an important occasion. If your horse is not comfortable, you are starting with a double whammy. He will be naturally concentrating on avoiding the discomfort, not the job in hand, and will inevitably not be able to give his best performance or, maybe, be on his best behaviour. So, having chosen the type of tack that suits your purpose, your priority is to put your horse's comfort first so that he can do his best for both of you.

Many countries have national organisations for training and qualifying people in the roles of making and fitting saddles, bridles and bits for the many purposes for which we employ horses. As time and research progress, it becomes more and more obvious that there is much more to designing and fitting tack than we ever imagined a generation ago. Entire books have been written about it, and national organisations often produce their own publications on their specialities to enlighten us all. Here, I can only cover the important basics of tack fit and use, concentrating on how it affects our horses, because tack really can make or break our partnership.

Thinking the right way about tack

Bridles were, obviously, invented so that humans could exert some control over their horses, although not all ancient peoples used them. Bits, again, came about to control horses, and nosebands were devised to use as an attachment for various straps like standing martingales and a version of side-reins. All these items, early 'gadgets', were intended to increase the horse's subjugation to man's requirements, and still are.

An old friend of mine and equestrian expert **par excellence**, Dr Sharon E. Cregier from Canada, says that her gauge of the quality of a horseman or woman is the amount or lack of clutter on their horse, particularly his head. I couldn't agree more. Returning to the point made twice already – that humans get rough and tough when they are desperate – increasing the amount of force and restriction used on a horse denotes very clearly a corresponding lack of skill, caring and competence in his rider, trainer or handler. 'Twas ever thus, and these days, although the amount of force and coercion our horses work under seems to increase, it is even more unnecessary than ever.

Why do I claim this? Even thousands of years ago, there were forms of riding we can call Classical. Ancient Greek cavalry commander, Xenophon, is the best-known early classical rider: indeed, I suppose he could be said to have first organised, set down and preached classical principles, but others used them individually and instinctively before him. As stated, horses do not respond well to cruelty, force and harshness any more than we do. Their natural way is to work as partners (that word again); they do best when they feel safe and confident with their partner whether human or equine, and true horsemen and women abhor harsh treatment of such a generous, sociable animal.

The brute-force type of horsemanship, although common, is unnecessary, as I claim, because effective, true classical principles and techniques are still alive and well and available in books ancient and modern, DVDs and variously online, and in a select group of **real** classical riders and trainers.

Not only that, but with the advent of equitation science about a couple of decades ago, we have **proven**, humane and successful methods of horsemanship readily available worldwide. It is a disgrace that our major equestrian organising bodies worldwide are largely ignoring it, and also real classical riding from my perception, but it will come as the horse world's 'social licence to operate' – or public sanction – comes increasingly under scrutiny.

Forceful methods and equipment designed and fitted to coerce horses into doing what their riders want, such as tight bridles and nosebands, severe bits and harsh riding techniques will have to be abandoned in favour of the humane training methods of true classical riding and equitation science: the two have much in common, both decrying harshness and promoting kind methods understandable to horses, and that work.

So, that was a bit of an offshoot but one which relates very much to the equipment, and its application, widely used on horses today. Now I am going to give some reliable guidelines to help you to help your horse, who will surely return your consideration and trouble through his well-being and performance.

Comfort is crucial

A horse's head is clearly covered with thin skin and there are many nerves running close up under it. It stands to reason, therefore, that any undue pressure on the head can easily cause discomfort and even pain. Nosebands in particular, in their myriad designs, can completely change the feel of a bridle and bit and help, hinder or hurt a horse. They can restrict breathing, swallowing of saliva and can prevent the horse relieving himself of bit pain by strapping his mouth closed. An open, mobile mouth and muzzle is a horse's way of communicating how he is feeling

Tack, Clothing and Protective Items

Figure 4.1: Most of us stretch out our horse's forelegs to smooth out the skin under the girth after saddling up, but there is a right way to do it. Note the handler's safe stance here. The leg is being supported below the knee and fetlock which makes the horse more comfortable and confident and is being extended correctly, out and down.

and of trying to ease himself. With a comfortable mouth, the horse is also better able to feel your messages via the bit.

The fit of a bridle should follow the old guidelines of comfort for the horse. Padded bridles may be intended to make them more comfortable, perhaps to partially compensate for the appalling current fashion and belief that bridles should be vice-tight, but they also make bridles stiff and clunky. A single or, maximum, double layer of leather, kept soft and supple, can move with your horse and is much more comfortable. The following advice on fit and adjustment may be unfamiliar to many modern riders, but they are correct and will be comfortable for your horse.

We should be able to easily slide a finger under all parts of a bridle. Around the ears, the headpiece and browband should be clear of the base of the ears, not rubbing or pressing up against them. The browband should follow the above guideline but should not be so loose that it flops around and irritates the horse. The throatlatch should permit the sideways width of a hand between it and the round jawbone.

Nosebands should be fitted in accordance with the wedge-shaped 'taper gauge' marketed and sold by the International Society for Equitation Science. This will allow a horse to swallow, breathe freely, move his jaws and open his mouth slightly. Alternatively, the noseband should allow two fingers width between it and the front bone of the horse's head – the nasal planum. A finger should slide easily along under any strap running along the chin groove.

The current fashion of using nosebands with dropped rear straps (into the chin groove) with bits having a curb chain or strap, which should also come well down into the chin groove, is a travesty of comfortable, effective bitting. If such restraint is needed, probably both horse and rider need better training.

Bridles should not press into or rub the base of the ears so the browband needs to be long enough to allow a generous fit. If the horse's poll conformation encourages the headpiece to lie too far forward, an individually designed one, probably with cutaways around the base of the ears, should be used. The cheekpieces of bridle and noseband must not lie too close to the corners of the eyes and the noseband must not rub up against, or even contact, the bottom of the sharp facial bones. The insides of the bridle straps need to be smooth and lie flat so as not to rub the horse's head. If the bridle is fitted too tightly or exerts too much pressure anywhere, remember that this might cause actual pain, either from skin rubs or pressure on nerves under the skin.

Bits are often fitted too high, pulling up the corners of the horse's mouth, causing discomfort, split skin, pain and ultimately insensitivity. Snaffle bits should create no more than one wrinkle here for comfort, depending on the position of the horse's teeth. Pelham and similar bits should just touch the corners of the mouth but not wrinkle them or hang down out of touch. Curb chains should hang down into the curb/chin groove and allow one finger to be slid underneath them. The use of a lip-strap is a personal decision, depending on the height of the upper cheek of the bit. For double bridles, the bridoon (thin snaffle) should create **one** wrinkle at the corners of the mouth and the curb bit should lie half an inch or a centimetre or so below it. In the mouth, the curb bit lies underneath the bridoon.

Another old saying: 'There is a bit for every man's head.' The choice of bits today is mind boggling and mostly quite unnecessary. If you need a bit for extra control, consider the kinder and more effective way first – better training. For what it is worth, generally my two favourite bits as an initial go-to for any horse or pony are firstly tasteless mouthpieces such as stainless steel, so you can be sure your horse doesn't dislike the taste in his mouth, no matter what the manufacturer says, and secondly there is no such thing as a 'warm' metal: if you want to warm your horse's bit hold it between your (clean) hands for a minute or two before using it.

For a good, comfortable snaffle bit I like a lozenge bit with shaped canons, with either eggbutt, loose ring or wire ring cheekpieces. Horses who have developed the habit of constantly champing at their bit, usually due to discomfort previously, settle better in an eggbutt whereas horses who tense their mouths and do not 'feel' the bit are encouraged to relax more with a loose or wire ring bit which is more movable.

For a curb-type bit, I like a simple half-moon pelham bit (not an arched pelham) with a smooth mouthpiece, no grooving. I have had a **lot** of success with these. There seems to be something about the way they hang on the horse's head that encourages him to drop his head and flex naturally very slightly even when dismounted. I find horses go kindly in these pelhams, quieten down if they have had mouth problems and accept a soft, in-touch, mutual contact with the rider's hands quite happily, all else being equal, that is, good riding and a comfortable horse.

I find it a good plan to give a horse a sugar-free mint immediately before putting the bit in and again immediately afterwards, as a routine. This gives the horse something pleasant to look forward to that stays with him for a while.

Saddles and girths are usually put on too far forward today, with the best intentions. It is believed that this helps get the rider more forward over the horse's centre of balance, which is about a hand's width behind the withers and two-thirds of the way down inside the chest directly below the spine. If we put on a saddle like this, it throws a well-designed and balanced saddle **out** of balance, tilts the pommel up, the cantle down and places the deepest part of the seat, where the rider's seat bones should be, towards the cantle, so defeating the object.

Also, the front of the saddle will then be too close to the tops of the shoulder blades. The shoulder blades swivel around a point about a third of the way down their length, so when a foreleg moves forward the top of the shoulder blade actually moves backward. Because the saddle is too far forward, this means the tops of the shoulder blades are impacted by the saddle and the horse's action interfered with at every stride, also potentially causing bruising there.

Another problem is that if the saddle is too far forward so will be the girth, pulling it forward into the elbow area, even if it is cut away behind the elbows depending on the horse's conformation, and causing bruising and pain here, too. With the saddle where it should be, so that you can fit the side of your hand between the top of the shoulder blade and the front of the saddle, this does not happen unless the horse has rather straight shoulders. (Horses with any conformation issue need saddles made especially for them.)

As for the rider's weight distribution when in the saddle, remember that the stirrup bars which take the stirrup leathers and, therefore, all the rider's weight in some gaits such as fast canter, gallop and jumping, are inevitably slightly in front of the rider's seat bones where his or her weight is concentrated (but not entirely) in other, 'full seat' gaits; that is, with the seat fully in the saddle, such as walk, sitting trot and a regular canter. In conventional rising trot, the rider's weight alternates between the seat of the saddle under his or her seat bones and the stirrup bars. See Chapter 6 for a better, classical way to do rising trot.

Saddle fitters are an invaluable aid to horses' comfort today. They undergo specialist training and are tasked with finding, or making, a saddle with panels that fit the horse underneath and a seat that fits the rider on top – no easy task, and there is the girth to fit, too. I know many people buy saddles online today, but it is generally not a good plan from your horse's viewpoint. There is **much** more to getting a saddle that fits than simply asking for the right length from front to back and 'small', 'medium' or 'large' from side to side. A great deal depends on the horse's action and conformation so, as it is such an important purchase, I should always recommend consulting a qualified saddle fitter. There are now qualifications for bridle fitters too, which is a great help.

Training aids are intriguing items that occupy a good deal of riders' time and imaginations but, once again, they are an admission of inadequate training. In a horse well-trained and well ridden, they are just not needed other than in truly exceptional circumstances. They are, of course, a means of strapping a horse up and tying him down, to 'persuade' or 'encourage' him to go

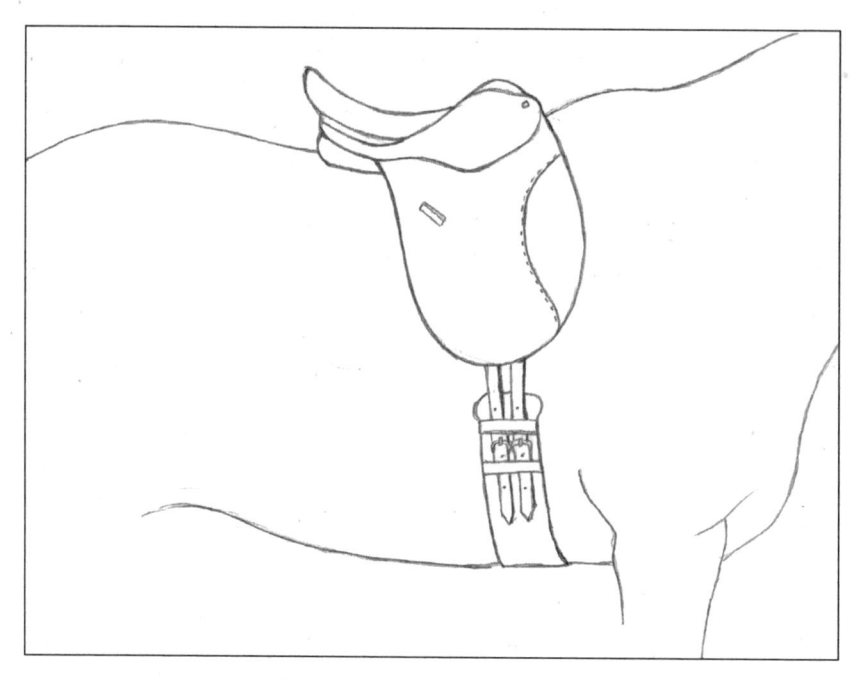

Figure 4.2: A well-fitting, flatwork-type saddle. It is set back far enough so that the fronts of the flaps come behind the tops of the shoulders (see text) but it does not press on the loins. This also enables the girth to lie well behind the elbows so that it does not press in here when the forelegs come back in their stride, so avoiding bruising and pain. Jumping saddles are trickier to fit, but the same rules need to apply, and it is a mistake to put on any saddle as far forward as most are today.

in a particular way or outline but the humane way to do this is through correct training (see Chapters 6 and 9).

You might come across a trainer who argues that positioning a horse in a particular way via training aids will not only mentally get him accustomed to going in that way, or outline, but also accustom his body to it so that he will 'grow into' or 'develop' into it. This is nonsense and betrays a lack of knowledge of equine biomechanics. It might produce results of a sort and quicker than doing it the right way, but it is certainly not a horse-friendly way of training and achieving correct results. It can certainly cause physical discomfort, even pain, mental confusion and distress and a lasting dislike of being ridden or worked in any way.

Can you imagine the outcry there would be if children at gymnastics or dancing classes were strapped into position by their teacher, or any show or display animals other than horses, in whose world alone it is considered the norm? Why is this so and why is it allowed? If you wouldn't like it yourself or if you wouldn't do it to your child, please don't do it to your horse or pony.

Protective items

Boots can play an important part in protecting our horses. Few people would work a horse loose, on the lunge or on long reins without boots all round, and many routinely hack out with boots of various sorts. There are working boots, travelling boots, knee pads, surgical boots, over-reach boots and various others. The main thing, especially with working boots, is to remember that they often get soil, grit and even little stones in them between the boot and the horse's legs which cause considerable irritation, soreness and even actual wounds. It's hard to tell till you use them but it's something to look out for. Over-reach boots need to be fitted carefully or their action can rub horses' pasterns raw.

It is most important that leg boots are fitted just tightly enough (maybe over padding) to keep them in place so that they don't slip down but not so tight as to cause discomfort or even injury. Pressure should be even all down the boot. They should be kept clean as they become hard and abrasive when dirty.

Rugs can be a boon or a curse to our horses. Again, you'll be familiar with the different types and what your horse needs, such as maybe a fly sheet in summer, a turnout rug and stable rug in winter, and you will probably need two of each so that you can keep them clean. Rug designs are positively ingenious today and rugs can be expensive, so it makes sense to see that they are properly designed to be horse-friendly so far as shape and fit are concerned, as well as serving their intended purpose.

A well-designed rug will be horse-shaped so far as the back seam is concerned, so that it rises at the front for the withers, dips smoothly for the back, rises again towards the croup and dips again to the root of the tail, or just beyond if it is an outdoor rug. A rug with a straight back seam cannot accommodate a horse's shape and must be uncomfortable, creating pressure at the withers and croup. The side-to-side shaping is also important, and good rugs have darts or pleats at elbow and stifle to accommodate the horse's body width. If they don't, they will certainly rub the shoulders and hips.

There is more to a well-fitting rug than its size, therefore, but to get your horse's size measure him from the middle of his chest, round his shoulder, along his side to just beyond the back of his thigh. Even so, a rug of the right size and with the design features described above may not fit your horse comfortably. As horses wear rugs for several or many hours, they **must** be comfortable otherwise the horses will be stressed all the time and may end up with rub and pressure sores. Most good manufacturers and dealers will let you try rugs, provided you return them, if necessary, clean and hairless!

The leg straps and 'harnesses' on modern rugs can be a bit complicated but usually do a good job. Just fit them so that you can get the sideways width of your hand between the strap and your horse: this should ensure they are close enough to keep the rug in place comfortably without risking the horse getting a leg in them but not so tight that they pull the rug out of place and cause discomfort.

My experience is that most people over-rug their horses, perhaps not realising that horses actually hate being too hot. They are also biologically much better equipped than we are to withstand cold temperatures provided they are properly acclimatised. What they hate is strong wind, heavy rain, insects and too much sun. In all of those cases, their field shelters will be put to good use. Most horses also dislike mud, or at least deep, wet mud and, of course, it is really bad to have their legs constantly exposed to it, white socks or not. Udder cream is a very good preventative where mud fever and general soreness are an issue.

Horses generally seem to love snow, and rolling and digging in it, and like rolling in soft sand (and the sea, as I remember well!). If you are in a position to do so, installing a sand pit for rolling would make you very popular with your horses. It's not very expensive, either. Some say the sand should not be sea-sand because its salty taste could encourage horses to eat it, but I was born and brought up by the sea and never found this – rolling yes,

Figure 4.3: A well-designed rug, following the shape of a horse's body. The front may seem a little low but fits well in front of the chest. The back seam follows the undulations of a horse's spine, the rug extends well down to give good protection, the back edge comes right back, even just past, the root of the tail, and the leg straps are just right, allowing the width of a hand between the strap and the rug for comfort plus security.

including under saddle if we didn't keep our wits about us – and in the sea itself – but nibbling the sand, never.

Saddle pads and cloths
Most people use cloths or numnahs these days, the important points being to keep them clean, free of anything that could cause soreness, and fresh, and make sure they are pulled well up into the saddle gullet so as not to press on the withers. Saddle pads, intended to modify the fit and feel of a saddle are a different matter. These can do a good job but can also cause another problem while correcting the original one.

For instance, a saddle pad system meant to raise the front of a saddle can upset the balance of the saddle so that it tilts and causes too much pressure at the back. They can also affect the side-to-side fit of a saddle and make it too tight. If you want to use a pad to correct your saddle, I think it would be good to discuss it with a saddle fitter first. It may just be best to have the saddle corrected.

5

How Horses Move Naturally
Why we Should Let Them

In this chapter:

- ❖ Our current situation and how horse and man came together.
- ❖ Make, shape and purpose.
- ❖ Natural movement of horses.
- ❖ Breeds and types.
- ❖ What poor modern riding does to horses' bodies and minds.
- ❖ The physical and mental advantages of horse-friendly methods of riding and groundwork.

If you love horses there is probably nothing you like more than watching them free in all their gaits, playing, bucking, leaping around, rearing, boxing, rolling, performing moves for which we have no names and generally cavorting around with their friends. It lifts our spirits as well as theirs and, perhaps, shows us beyond doubt what they are capable of when left to themselves – how stunning and beautiful they are, how exciting and uplifting not to mention entertaining and moving. I'd much rather watch that than any modern dressage or showing display.

It also shows us how much we change our horses' natural ways of going when we 'school' or 'train' them, give them marks for abandoning nature's way and sublimating themselves to us in walking, trotting and cantering, not to mention jumping, and doing all sorts of manoeuvres they would hardly ever do, if at all, left to themselves. The human idea of a horse isn't anything like as good as their own.

Until a generation or two ago, the idea of riding and schooling horses was to achieve in the ridden horse the best **natural** gaits of which a horse was capable but under the weight and at the request, not the demand, of a rider. If you want to see a brilliant example of this, search online for the gold medal-winning French Thoroughbred, Taine, ridden by Commandant Xavier Lesage in the 1932 Olympics. You will also come across other riders of a similar ilk and will see what was genuine, original dressage, as a test of horsemanship. When I watch Taine I cry for what we have lost. It is not that I am living in the past but that horsemanship in general has moved away from its purpose and principles, to the detriment, in my view and many other people's, of the horses. And today's riders don't know what they're missing.

Simply remembering that aim – to reproduce the horse's best, individual way of going under a rider – it makes you wonder **why** various aspects of competition riding have changed not only some horses' ways of going, but brought us to purposely change even their conformation and the action they are born with, as well as the techniques embedded in much modern riding instruction.

The action and conformation some competition and show horses have today, around the world, is a corruption of what a good, sound, capable and healthy horse should be and, of course, changing what animals are and, therefore, what they can do does not only happen in the horse world. Conscientious veterinary surgeons and others have, for decades now, been complaining about it but it seems that nothing definite is ever done to correct it.

How did it all start?

It is not beyond the bounds of our imagination to consider what was passing through the minds of our ancestors around 6,000 or more years ago when they saw wild horses living their wild lives, and realising how fast some of them were, how strong some appeared to be and how comfortable their backs looked compared with other large species. As they started capturing young or injured horses and ponies and confining them for meat, blood and milk, tethering mares, perhaps, for mating by wild stallions and getting to know how to manage horses, domestic herds would build up and need managing. Perhaps some bright, young spark one day jumped up on to the back of a horse to reach some other point, liked the feel of it, and riding was born. We believe, though, that horses were used for pulling **travois** and sledges before that, and pulling felled trees as they cleared land for habitation and, eventually, farming. Once the wheel was invented humans never looked back. Horses were stronger, faster and more trainable than oxen, although both were often used, but the horse's unique attributes soon made him indispensable.

Make, shape and purpose

People have for thousands of years bred horses for their own purposes. When a specific, sole purpose has been the aim, such as speed as in the racehorse or pulling power as in heavy draught horses, a specific type good at that task presents itself as a by-product, not with human intention, and becomes recognisable. Not unreasonably, early peoples must have noticed that animals' characteristics were passed on to their offspring and realised the possibilities and advantages of getting horses of the same type to mate together for a particular role, or of different types to mate together for a different role, or of 'creating' in-between types, and so it carried on.

Usually we do no harm to the horses, unless we do silly things like purposely breeding for a disadvantageous feature because it appeals to some people, but which could actually weaken our horses. Once humans realised the almost limitless advantages of all those different features in one species, they started to manipulate what **we**, not nature, decreed was a good example of a horse (or other animal) for the job, and that's when things started to go wrong for the animals.

How horses move naturally

The basic four gaits of horses are, of course, walk, trot, canter and gallop. Horses spend most of their movement time walking around foraging and meeting up with other herd members. Trot speeds up getting from one spot to another, canter is used largely for moving from one area to another, say when looking for fresh grazing, and gallop is **the** gait used to escape from predators or anything else frightening. The faster a horse goes the slightly more forward is his centre of balance and all the gaits are different in order of footfalls and the rider's need to sit to them – to change his or her weight distribution, way of sitting or half-sitting and way of positioning and using their body to stay with the horse and control him. Ideally, a horse needs straight, true action, that is, his hind legs should follow exactly the flight path of his forelegs so that, when watching him from directly in front or behind, you can only see two legs. Irregular beats can indicate lameness and deviations from the flight path indicate conformational faults that could cause soundness or work problems.

Walk: This is known as a four-time gait in that four regular and even beats are easily distinguishable by sound and feel. The legs move individually, of course, say left hind, left fore, right hind and right fore, repeating. There is no moment of suspension when the horse is entirely in the air.

Figure 5.1: Here, an 'impure' walk is shown, as can occur when a horse is excited or is being pushed to walk too fast by the rider or handler.

Trot: This is a two-time gait in which diagonal pairs of legs move in turn, say left hind and right fore together, then right hind and left fore together. There is a moment of suspension between each beat as the diagonals pass each other in the air and the horse springs from one to the other.

Canter: A three-time gait starting with one hind foot and finishing with its opposite fore foot, so left hind, right hind and left fore together, and finally right fore. The horse naturally canters with the left fore 'leading' or 'pointing the way' (actually landing last) when going to the left and vice versa. Although horses are perfectly able to canter on what riders call 'the wrong leg', in other words landing the right fore last when bearing left, and vice versa. After the third beat, the horse is in suspension in the air.

Figure 5.2: The trot is a two-beat gait. Here the right diagonal is in support on the ground and the left in flight through the air. If the horse were being ridden on a right curve, the rider would be rising just now, and vice versa. There is a moment of suspension in the air as the horse springs up between the diagonals.

A 'disunited canter' means that the horse gets his sequence of footfalls in canter wrong – he might start with his left hind, then his right hind but, instead of his left fore accompanying the right hind, his right fore lands next just after the right hind, and finally his left fore lands, and vice versa. This is usually pretty uncomfortable for the rider, who is rocked from side to side: it usually happens due to pain or discomfort, or to a poorly balanced and positioned rider interfering with the horse's action.

Gallop: This is a 'spread-out' canter, with four separate rapid beats, say left hind, right hind, left fore and finally right fore, and vice versa, a moment of suspension occurring after the leading fore makes the final beat. The 'break' in the footfall sequence comes in what would be the second canter beat, that is in this example, between the right hind and the left fore.

How Horses Move Naturally

Figure 5.3: The canter is a three-beat gait. Here the left fore is about to land so the horse is said to be in left canter. If he were being ridden, the right way to sit this would be for the rider to have his or her left seat bone and shoulder slightly forward to accord with the position of the horse's back during most of the stride, and vice versa. That positioning is most comfortable for the horse and is all the confirmation he needs to stay in canter. (See text.) There is a moment of suspension after the leading fore foot leaves the ground, during which the horse can change legs, if appropriate.

It is interesting to observe horses at liberty 'changing legs' in canter and gallop, or doing what we call a 'flying change'. Many riders struggle with this movement but horses do it quite naturally in canter and even flat-out gallop, as can be seen if you watch racing. When they have trouble doing it with a rider, it is almost always **because** of the rider being unbalanced, positioned badly or being too active and hassling the horse. More on this in Chapter 9.

All equines are naturally 'forehand heavy', that is, they carry most weight, very roughly two-thirds depending on breed and type, on their forehands, so their forelegs come in for a good deal of stress and are mainly used for weight-bearing, having to carry the front part of the torso, the forehand and also the weight of the head and neck, whereas the hind legs are meant more for propulsion.

Jumping: The jumping ability, talent even, of some horses is probably a throwback to when their ancestors lived in forests. Those who could hop over fallen tree trunks could get around better and escape predators easier than those who found them an obstruction.

The horse's natural jumping action is to approach the jump, let's say from canter, the gait horses prefer to jump from, although this is not always the case. He will approach with a foreleg leading, drop his head a little while he judges the height and, if visible, the depth from front to back of the obstacle. When he judges his take-off distance to be reached, he plants both his hind feet together side by side, rears up his forehand, lifting his forelegs up from the shoulders and elbows and bending them at the knees, straightening out his hind legs as he pushes his body up and over the obstacle.

Crucially, his head and neck stretch fully out and forward and he 'jumps around his head': that is, his head stays more or less at the same level moving over the ground, while his body tackles the obstacle. His forehand rises up and over the jump, then his body levels out through the top of the flight, next the forehand starts to drop and the hindquarters rise, with tucked up hind legs, over the obstacle. He will land on one foreleg, let's say the right, the left follows smoothly landing well in front of it, his body and hindquarters, with tucked hind legs, level out and his forefeet lift off the ground for a split second as the first hind leg, the right in this example, lands followed by the left.

The natural jumping action of horses today is very frequently considerably restricted by their riders in a modern jumping technique that has developed over the past several decades and which is discussed in Chapter 10.

Breeds and types

There are hundreds of breeds and types of horse and pony in the world now. My artist for this book, and several of my others, Maggie Raynor, and I present in this chapter her drawing of a lovely type of riding horse for you to look at and get the idea of good, balanced riding conformation and type. The Thoroughbred, whose main job is racing, plays a large part in most of the lighter types, whether for riding or driving. The now-popular regional and national warmbloods all have a large helping of Thoroughbred blood in them, mated with local breeds and types. In fact, the Thoroughbred itself is strictly a warmblood because it is a mixture of mainly 'hot', Oriental blood such as the Arabian and the Barb and 'common' or 'cold' blood such as heavier-type horses and ponies. Rather obviously, hot-blooded horses and cold-blooded horses and ponies, as described earlier, evolved in hot and colder parts of Europe, Arabia and Asia, developing features to enable them survive in those areas.

The Thoroughbred's full name is The English Thoroughbred because it was 'made in England' but from largely foreign parts! It is now bred and mixed up with its own bloodlines almost all over the world where horses are valued and is a truly international breed.

Some of the loveliest horses on the planet are Anglo-Arabs, 'Anglo' in this case denoting English Thoroughbred blood. They add an extra dash of soundness, spirit, and beauty to the Thoroughbred, and the French have made a speciality of breeding them.

Classical riders often prefer the Iberian horses from Portugal and Spain, which existed long before the Thoroughbred was created. They certainly have the carriage and fire with docility, compactness and strength, usually with lovely temperaments, needed for classical training and riding. The famous Lipizzaner horses of the Spanish Riding School in Vienna are based on Iberian breeds, mainly the Spanish Andalusian, now termed the Pura Raza Española (PRE) or pure-blood Spanish.

British native ponies in all their varieties and breeds are extremely popular for children and smaller adults, and take very well to riding or driving. They are exported all over the world but often seem to me to lose 'type' in other countries.

Whatever type or breed of equine you prefer, natural or 'manufactured', the main points of conformation and action apply – balanced body with straight action. If breed enthusiasts breed for what are essentially faults, as mentioned above, be aware that they can adversely affect the animal's health and soundness, not to mention its well-being.

Modern riding techniques

It may be surprising to note that some of the best conformed horses in the world are horses not bred for how they look but how fast they can gallop, and sometimes jump at speed – racehorses. The superb conformation of most Thoroughbred horses has come about for the old reasons of that being incidental and what their jobs produce, because ability, not looks, is still the most sought-after quality in the Thoroughbred world. Thoroughbreds do have faults; as a breed they are not noted for having the best of feet and their sensitive, autocratic temperaments are often not suited to nervous, 'unquiet' or domineering riders. Warmbloods, I was told when they first became fashionable, are not so reactive, often sounder and 'put up with a lot', but today more and more Thoroughbred blood is being used in some Warmblood breeds to harvest their qualities of toughness along with the sensitivity, flair and that 'look-at-me' quality so sought after in modern competitions.

It can be a tricky balancing act, though, because modern riding techniques have, from my perspective, become harsher over recent decades. A firm, unrelenting bit contact has become almost universal to achieve the look of a horse on the bit and collected, even if, to a skilled eye, he is neither. An enforced way of going results in subtle and sometimes obvious 'evasions' by the horse – self-defensive actions and ways of going to relieve the considerable discomfort imposed upon him.

This sort of pulling and holding in from the front has repercussions throughout the horse's body. He cannot balance or move at all naturally when so constrained. His vision is restricted unless he is able, and can sustain, 'looking up' all the time just to see where he is going, because his head is being pulled, or carried out of acquired habit, in and down. This pressure from the front causes him to take too much weight back on to his hindquarters, whereas this should only be happening by means of initial, correct training and work to strengthen his hindquarters to accept such weight.

Some horses can be seen to be on a rigid type of contact, but others, also going in this way, are clearly on a fairly light rein which, itself, looks good, but they have been schooled at home to go like this – I can only imagine that it is to avoid criticism.

Pretty much the horse's whole body is likely to be subjected to discomfort and pain, from his mouth to his back legs, due to unnatural stresses on his body – his muscles, soft tissues and bones. Being made to be used in an unnatural way often for extended periods of time during training, the tissues can be injured which, of course, causes the horse aches and pains, to the point at which it can be difficult to keep the horse in work.

The standard and famous stipulation of how a horse should go under saddle is with the poll the highest point of his outline (excepting the ears, of course) and his weight carried voluntarily by him back a little more on to his hindquarters, which makes moving his forehand easier for him, particularly in bending and lateral work. This should be achieved by means of correct training, not force. However, at just about every competitive equestrian gathering, whether training or competing, almost all the horses' heads are bowed down and the fronts of their faces behind a vertical, imaginary line dropped from their foreheads to the ground, known as being 'behind the vertical' or 'BTV'. Their highest point is about a third of the way along the neck usually. Their necks look shortened in relation to the rest of their bodies and their throats cramped and wrinkled, indicating constriction here which hampers breathing and swallowing saliva, hence the copious froth which may be present. (No, froth is not a good thing; a moist mouth is.) Strained facial expressions and thrashing tails betray the horses' predicament.

Their action, particularly at the 'higher' levels of some competitions, can be artificially flashy in front, looking almost like a poor version of Spanish trot. When a horse is going well, the angle of the forearm and the rear cannon bones should be the same, yet the forearms are often too near the horizontal. The flicking action of the forelegs shown by horses being driven too fast and on the forehand, with the toe flicking up and the foot landing often incorrectly heel first, can strain the tendons and ligaments in the leg, and, as the back in this artificial action cannot be arched up beneath the rider in a strong posture, back and pelvic-area injuries are likely.

When the horse takes his weight back on to inadequately strengthened hindquarters, again injuries can occur in the hind legs, particularly the hocks but also the entire length of the back is susceptible.

I understand, from a like-minded vet, that these types of injuries are, in his experience, the cause of competition horses retiring or even being put down earlier than in the past, and more of the males being kept entire so that then they can at least be taken advantage of for breeding.

It is easy to imagine what effects this constantly having to put up with pain and hard riding has on the horses' mental health. It may be hard to prove, though, but experienced and caring horse people can tell what is happening. I am certain, from my own observations, that many of the stereotypies shown by harshly trained and unnaturally kept horses are due to their lifestyles. I remember going to try a former dressage horse and, latterly, showjumper, which didn't know me yet and cowered to the back of his box when I entered with his tack. I had met him previously, minus tack, and found him rather suspicious but not afraid, but when I returned later with the tack he was clearly expecting to be given a bad time by a human, as must have been usual for the poor boy. Horses in this kind of lifestyle must live miserable lives of what amounts to mental and physical torture, all for the sake of human ambition, and my heart goes out to all of them.

The good news!
Having got the bad stuff out of the way, I promise not to mention it again. There is plenty of good news to come, all of it achievable and uplifting for horses and riders, and **so** very rewarding for both. A word of warning, though. Some horses and ponies who have been abused, even unknowingly, possibly due to their riders simply doing what some trusted instructor has told them, can be rehabilitated but it can take a long time. If the horse encounters similar conditions or techniques again, symptoms may reoccur. Sadly, in some cases, they may never recover. They may be prone to defending themselves in ways that are very dangerous to us, such as biting, kicking or crushing us against a wall or knocking us over and trampling us, or by rearing and bucking when ridden to try to get rid of us. If you are planning to buy a horse you don't know, try to find someone you really trust to assess him and spend time watching him and how he reacts to everything. I feel that mentally harmed horses are not suitable for most amateur riders because they may well defend themselves in dangerous ways even before anyone lays a finger on them. Horses have **very** good memories.

Can horses be happy?

There was some debate in the horse world a while ago, among vets, equine scientists and horse owners and riders as to whether or not horses can actually experience happiness. My own feeling is that yes, of course they can, and anyone emotionally close to a horse or pony knows instinctively whether he is happy, or is sad, depressed, feels ill, is angry, frightened, worried or any of many other emotions. Happiness is a priceless gift to us all. From a scientific viewpoint, it is known that mental and physical health and well-being improve in leaps and bounds when a person's life improves, and surely any animal lover recognises the same effect in their animals. Unlike humans, we cannot directly ask an animal if he or she is happy, but we can tell by the animal's behaviour, demeanour, appearance and response to his world whether he is happy or not. To suggest that happiness cannot be experienced by animals is, to me, like going back to the times when all animals were generally called 'dumb animals', meaning insensitive and a bit stupid, not capable of emotions. (Having said that, it is only fairly recently that the British government has admitted that animals are 'sentient' – capable of emotional and physical feelings – and passed it into law.)

In all the ways in which we interact with our horses, our aim is usually to get them to do what we want, not least for safety. We ride them, do groundwork with them, we groom and care for them, we teach them new movements, some of us teach them tricks and how to obey verbal words and maybe our body language and hand signals as well. No matter what we do with them, if we do it in ways they can understand and do not make them feel uncomfortable, browbeaten or cause them pain, if we are consistent with rewards and praise and make our horse confident in us, it builds on our partnership and they can enjoy it greatly. Likewise, if our horse is really not cut out for certain things, we need to not force him to do them but find something he can excel at and enjoy.

Positive emotions like happiness, confidence and contentment trigger the flow of 'happy hormones' around the body, which are known to both protect and heal mind, body and spirit. The medical and veterinary professions recognise that health improves all round when creatures human and animal experience positive states. We thrive rather than just survive, and we both get the best out of each other. This applies to **all** aspects of our horses' lives so we need to remember what they need when we aren't there so far as friends, food, accommodation, freedom, safety and the facility to be a horse are concerned. These comprise the greatest time-portion of their lives, not their time with us, but horses really do recognise us as a welcome source of everything they need, and as protection from the bad things in life. Some people may scoff at this but it **is** true. Animals in general are far more perceptive, knowing and understanding than many people think.

6

Co-operation, not Domination
Riding **With** Your Horse, not Against Him

In this chapter:

- ❖ Acquiring a horse- and human-friendly seat, position and balance, and the difference it makes.
- ❖ Riding with your seat.
- ❖ The right contact – you **can** find it.
- ❖ Applying effective, humane aids with bit, legs and whip.

Horses are great creatures for not exerting themselves too much most of the time. Their basic take on life, for most of them, is relaxation, enjoyment – especially eating, cosying up to friends, having the odd spurt of energy now and then, playing, rolling around, lying down, dozing, sleeping, being comfortable, feeling free – stuff like that.

As a teacher of classical riding (a pretty relaxed form of riding) for over twenty years, combined with equitation science for most of it, the main fault that I have found needs correcting first in riders is that they **do** too much. I don't know if this is due to the pace and concerns of modern life, because someone (a teacher)

Co-operation, not Domination

is watching them, because they think they have constantly to be correcting and directing their horse, or what. I do know that once I explain the ethos of classical riding and the absolute clarity of equitation science, plus reminding them of how being laid back is the main state of mind of the horse species, things start to get better. When the riders have managed to calm themselves down, stop fiddling and pay more attention to how their horse **is** than what they expect him to do, everything improves like magic.

Riding **with** your horse, rather than setting your mind and body against him, treating him like a friend and partner rather than a vehicle, and asking him to do things and making suggestions rather than ordering him around is quite unusual from my observations. A very effective way of getting with this way of thinking is to put yourself in your horse's place, inside his differently shaped body from yours, and, if possible, thinking about the things that matter to him.

For a start, we need to accept that horses do not have the kind of social hierarchy that humans have. They do not have ranking systems, bosses and inferiors or a clear top-to-bottom status sphere. True, some horses are better at getting their own way over others, but not **all** others. As mentioned earlier, there is no herd 'big boss' everyone obeys, there are individual friendships and associations, and horses they prefer to stay away from, but horse-herd society is not like normal primate behaviour (and we are primates, of course). Some owners brag about their horse being boss of the herd or bemoan the fact that he or she is bottom of the heap, but this is putting a human spin on how things work in **equine** society and misjudging the real situation. Let me tell you a true story to illustrate this.

At a fairly large livery yard set up on a farm as a profitable diversification, very common today, there lived an old mare who was regarded by horses and humans as of the lowest status of the horses. None of the others bothered with her much nor she with them. She was always out of it, a little way from the others, as often happens with sick horses, or old ones coming down in life. She was quiet, minding her own business, not hassled and not hassling. She seemed quite content, or maybe resigned.

One day, a bullock broke into the horses' paddock from his field, running around and testing the horses' reactions, snorting at them, charging and halting before a collision, but clearly very keen on making his mark. The dozen or so horses were naturally alarmed and started milling around in a bit of a panic, splitting up, running hither and thither and not knowing what to do. No one took charge and the situation was looking grim as the bullock became more and more assertive.

After only a minute or so, the old mare, who had been watching quietly from some distance away, went over to the other horses, gathered them together and, by her body language, told them to stay back. They obeyed her implicitly. Then she turned to the bullock, keeping herself between him and them. She arched her neck, snorted and reared up in his face, waving her forefeet at him. He stopped in his tracks, looked amazed but tried a little charge at her. She reared again and squealed, and again. She drove him to the broken rail in the fence but by that time the farmer had seen what was going on and came to sort things out. He put the bullock back in his field while the old mare watched until he was safely secured. Then she turned back to the other horses who had all stayed exactly where she had put them. She looked at them and must have communicated to them 'It's OK now, as you were.' And they calmly resumed grazing.

So, an 'inferior' old lady, whom the bullock could have easily flattened and injured, and of whom the other horses never took any notice, took control of the situation, of the large, strong, young bullock and of the horses in no uncertain terms. She exerted her wisdom, authority and intelligence, quickly assessed the situation and took charge. She undoubtedly prevented injuries, and waited till she was satisfied that the human had tied up the loose ends before going back to her grazing. Peace restored.

So, if we accept that horses are not like us socially but have a much more even society, perhaps we can more easily get rid of the 'show him who's boss' culture that is so common now, and consider that asking clearly and reasonably is highly likely to get the result you want. Some horses react quite strongly against being **told** firmly and determinedly, and many instructors regard asking as weakness. 'You have to show him who's boss or he'll never do anything for you, and that's not safe' is a very common instruction, or reason, for harsh rather than more polite ways of getting your way and of giving aids, usually called cues or signals in equitation science. It's also a good idea to be prepared to allow for a horse not being **able** to comply or having a good reason, such as fear or confusion, not to do something, which will need looking into.

Asking rather than demanding also does not mean that you usually have to take 'no' for an answer. Very few horses seek to 'walk all over you' if you ask in a way they understand. Most horses are happy to have a relationship with humans similar to the one with their herd mates – and that is, indeed, a partnership or fairly equal friendship. Some people we get on with, some we don't: it's the same with horses between their own kind, and we both work the same way with creatures of another species. Horses want to be treated fairly and so do we and both species understand that.

Your seat, position and balance
Doing less and opening yourself up to your horse is, then, an excellent start to building a better and more complying relationship with your horse – you comply with his needs, and he complies with your requests – a sound partnership. The classical seat is your means of achieving that when riding because it gives

you a really horse-friendly seat, position and balance when riding. The three illustrations in this chapter, with their explanatory captions, will give you a visual guide to proven, more effective and actually safer (because more secure) seats in, or just out of, the saddle.

The basic, flatwork, classical seat is still the best and I am happy to stick my neck out and say that it will never be bettered. In this book we also discuss its versions for faster gaits and jumping. The whole ethos of any true classical seat is to keep the horse comfortable, working at ease, under control and, above all, **unconstrained** commensurate with his being guided. The way to do this is, first and foremost, to create the most perfect balance you can, and it is easier than you think. That is the basis of the classical seat: your seat and position create your balance, and doing only as much as is needed makes it easier to maintain. Riders who are over-active lose their position and balance easily and they irritate and distract their horses. Riders who use hard, coercive aids lose their balance easily because they destroy relaxation and correct positioning in their own bodies and create blocks, therefore they cannot go **with** their horse's movement and the horse has to try to compensate for a contrary rider working against him.

Can you imagine what it must be like to be a horizontally balanced animal with a top-heavy, vertically balanced one on your back, moving about, swinging around, sometimes going against your own balance or even almost, or actually, bringing you down? It must be quite frightening because horses' first instinct is self-preservation and staying on their feet is crucial to that. Horses can perform the most demanding and intricate movements beautifully **if** their riders are in ideal balance with them. The modern style of riding can be rather stiff, which blocks body language between horse and rider both ways. Stiffness makes aids crude and imprecise instead of subtle and tactful. The reverse is a sloppy rider, insecure even if experienced, moving around and, so, giving the horse pressures he might interpret as aids or which he simply has to counteract with his body to stay in balance himself. No wonder so many horses are distracted, discouraged and defensive. They have to work against all this and it's so much more difficult than it need be.

Acquiring 'the seat'

This section tells you how to acquire, firstly, the basic classical flatwork seat which is the basis of the others. The first difference you will notice is the relaxation and security you will feel, the second how much easier it is to get through to your horse and get results and, thirdly, you will be much more sensitive to what your horse is doing underneath you and what he is 'telling' you by his actions.

First, mount your horse. This is best done from a high mounting block, a wall, a rock, whatever you can find, that is high enough so that you can stand on it and just put a leg over the horse without needing to use a stirrup. If you use a stirrup in the normal way it unavoidably creates a lot of uncomfortable sideways pressure on the far side of the horse's back as the saddle is pulled into it, and on the saddle. Otherwise, try to find someone to pull down quite hard on the opposite stirrup to even up the pressure on the horse's back as you mount, if you have no other choice.

The flatwork seat, figure 6.1 in this chapter, shows what is probably a familiar picture and what we must aim at. The strange thing is that, although many people know about it and see it illustrated in books, few really try to adopt it. Or they genuinely think that they **are** in that seat but aren't really. We get so used to the feel of how we normally ride that we can't tell what we are really doing, so it's a big help to have mirrors available or the reflective glass of a large window to keep an eye on yourself.

Figure 6.1: The classical seat for flatwork. Note the straight, vertical line which runs ear > shoulder > elbow/hip > ankle, not down the back of the heel. This is because the flexible ankle joint helps to absorb the weight of the rider. With the seat bones in the centre of the seat of a well-fitting saddle, this seat is the best-balanced and most adaptable position for all flatwork, fast work and jumping, including racing.

So, you're in the saddle. Take up the reins on a very light, or no, contact. It's helpful to have a neck strap. If your horse is in the habit of moving off at once, maybe expecting that instruction from you, gently halt and keep him at halt if he tries to move. He needs to relax and stand still waiting for you to give the walk-on aid. Don't nag or hold him, just ask him to stand, release the contact and let him relax. Your new seat will help him with this.

Co-operation, not Domination

Sit in your saddle with your feet out of your stirrups and – keep telling yourself this all the time – **stretch up from your waist and drop down from your waist.** That is the tricky part for most conventional riders who are not taught to sit **in** the saddle. Completely relax your seat and leg muscles as though you had no use in them for now, letting your legs and toes hang lifelessly down. Stretch your upper body, gently but definitely, straight up from the waist to the top of your head, keeping your elbows back at the **sides** of your hips (your upper arms, therefore, absolutely vertical, as when you are standing up). Let your lower body drop down from your waist and your legs, too.

Now feel with your two seat bones (the lowest part of your pelvis) to make sure they are in the lowest part, the dip, of your saddle seat. Just sit there feeling all this and get used to it. Stretch up, drop down, elbows **back** at the **sides** of your hips, legs lifeless, toes dropping down. That's right! Well done!

Another key phrase to remember is 'controlled relaxation'. Your upper body is held but not forced upright (copy the drawing), in controlled relaxation, your lower body and legs soft and dropped around your saddle and your horse's sides. This might feel strange at first but stick with it. Get a friend to put their hand between your calf and your horse's side and pull your leg sideways away (keep your knee down), then remove their hand. Your leg should flop lifelessly down again. If it doesn't, you are not relaxing it. Try again, both legs, till you get the feel of 'dead legs'.

Next, have your helper lead you around in walk, if possible, or give an **inward** squeeze with your inner calves – repeat, inner calves, not by raising your heels – and just feel your horse's back moving and dipping from side to side and each hind leg alternately pushing your loose seat up as it hits the ground and pushes off. If you can't feel it you are not loose enough. **Do not** let your shoulders rock from side to side with the rhythm, a very common fault: hold them still and, so, non-interfering, in that controlled relaxation and let your seat do its job of absorbing and feeling the movement. The dividing point is your waist which acts as a loose, absorbing join between upper and lower body.

Sitting like this, you will start to understand balance. Your upper body is helping you and your horse: keep it still, up and out of it, in controlled relaxation. Your seat is how you will, pretty soon, communicate with your horse.

Now try a little sitting jog, just enough to keep your horse going. With a correctly relaxed seat and waist you won't bounce up and down but mould softly to your saddle. It takes practice but is essential and so worthwhile. It is crucial that you don't upset your horse by letting your hands go up and down with his movement, hence the neck strap. Your upper body is being held in controlled relaxation, remember, in your impeccable classical seat and vertical position. Don't rely on the neck strap **too** much. You can do it!

Don't forget to change reins. The crunch point of how 'feeling' your seat has become is that you will be able to call out to your friend, watching you from a distance, which hind foot is landing when. Think of your horse's back as a table with a leg at each corner. When a back foot leaves the ground the table/back loses its support and dips. Your loose seat will feel that, if not at first. Then its pair will do the same, so your pelvis **only** and **not** your shoulders will be rocking gently from side to side, and you will, with practice, if you keep your seat properly relaxed, be able to feel this and call out 'left, right, left, right' as your horse goes along. Then promote yourself to sitting trot and call out the hind footfalls again. When you can do this reliably, you've got it. It will take a few sessions. (The reason you need to be able to do this is because

Co-operation, not Domination

Figure 6.2: The classical seat for rising trot positions the rider's shoulders above her knees. This enables her to tilt her pelvis forward in a discreet rise, and allow gravity to bring her down again, maintaining her upper body position – a much less disruptive trot than the conventional, upright 'up-down' action, and more comfortable and reassuring for the horse.

the best moment to give an aid for a different gait or movement is when the hind leg starting it is in the air: if the required foot is on the ground bearing weight, it cannot initiate an aid.)

You can progress from being led to being lunged if you can find someone reliable to lunge you – on a **large** circle and not fast in each gait: your horse should walk out and trot steadily. A large circle is particularly important when you canter so that the horse does not feel he has to lean in to stay balanced. After giving any leg aid, resume the relaxation. Try to give the aids with the insides of your calves, certainly not by raising your heels and using the backs of them.

To start canter, make sure you are stretched up and dropped down, place your inside seat bone and shoulder slightly forward and give the aid with your outside leg slightly back, inside leg supporting, ideally when the outside hind foot is lifting. In canter only, you keep your inside seat bone and shoulder forward according to which leg your horse is on, and on straight lines or curves. You will not believe how much this will help your horse to get, and stay on, the correct leg. So, in left canter, left fore leading, your left seat bone and shoulder will be forward all the time, and vice versa. Relax into it. If you stiffen up so will your horse.

The correct seat, position and balance

Have the classical flatwork position in your mind all the time and practise the above techniques with your controlled relaxation. You will help your horse no end riding like this. You are central, vertical, and absorbing his movements with your seat and waist. Generally, your legs drop down into the stirrups with – look at the drawing – the balls of your feet on the stirrup treads and your ankle joints – **not** the backs of your heels – below your knee joints on the straight line. This will help to stabilise your balance and keep your legs where they are best placed.

It is often taught that you should 'go with' your horse's inclination or 'tilt' when cornering in faster gaits. Please don't do this. We are top-heavy on our horse's back and any slight movement is magnified on his back. I have seen horses brought down by riders leaning over with the horse in faster gaits, thinking they are helping. If you search barrel racing online, you will see that the horses' bodies are often at a 45-degree angle but their riders are vertical: if they weren't they would both crash down. It's the same principle with 'ordinary' riding. Stay as helpfully vertical as you can to help your horse stay on his feet.

Figure 6.3: A common sight in conventional, modern riding. This horse is upset and really struggling as his head and facial expression show. The rider is stiff and braced against his movement instead of being in controlled relaxation, going with his movement and supporting him. The bit contact is too firm, restrictive, unrelenting and probably painful, and the swishing tail gives away the horse's anger and distress.

Riding with your seat

Conventional, modern riders are quite obsessed with using their hands. We, as primates, are a very 'handy' species, but that is no good when we are trying to be good riders and friends to our horses. We should aim to keep a light, in-touch contact, and a stable bit in our horse's mouth that we only move when giving a message to him. That is the essence of the famous 'good hands'. It makes our messages clear and prevents our irritating and distracting the horse at other times. It also means we can feel any message our horse sends to us up the reins. We need to ride with the focus of our balance and security – our seats. Our hands can almost be an afterthought, distributing the effects of our seat and legs.

Chapter 9 covers the exact techniques of using your seat to send messages and ask for various movements, but if you can centre your attention on your seat and dropped legs rather than your hands, you will find riding with your seat, like all the best classical riders, becomes second nature. It will also centre your and your horse's attention on your balance on his back and become your control headquarters – a much more co-operative and friendly way to ride than pulling with your reins all the time, kicking or spurring your horse, and not being aware of just how disturbing to a horse an uncontrolled seat in their rider can be.

The classical jumping seat

The classical jumping seat (see Chapter 10) is very different from the modern jumping seat. It is a horse-friendly adaptation of the flatwork seat we have just studied, taught as standard until a few decades ago (and not because jumps then were easier because they weren't). It keeps everything minimal, balance-centred and as still as possible while interfering with the horse's efforts as little as possible as he, in his generosity, carries us over. He's the one doing the jumping, not us, and we need to let him by giving him freedom, being in balance with him and 'keeping our mouths shut', as a teacher of mine used to say long ago. Present him to the jump and let him get on with it without interference.

The light seat

There are various, slightly different versions of this, but basically the image shown on page 174, figure 10.1, is it. It is used for faster gaits from a swinging-on canter to a flat-out gallop and is good to use between obstacles, although many riders today adopt an upright seat for that: it is not quite so easy to adopt a classically based upright seat with the shorter stirrups used for jumping but so long as the rider does not bang his seat on the horse's back or harass his mouth, I'll accept it.

The balance in the light seat is shoulder above elbow above knee above toes, broadly speaking. This forward lean from the hip joints, not the waist, and with **back flat**, gives the rider good body control and, as you might imagine, still relies on your controlled relaxation to help you and your horse.

Co-operation, not Domination

In any forward, light seat, the rider's weight is taken mainly on the feet in the stirrups, of course, but where is that weight felt by the horse? Because the weight runs up the stirrup leathers which are supported by the stirrup bars, our weight is taken by the stirrup bars and, so, down on to two very small areas of the horse's back just behind and on either side of the withers. To lessen this concentration of weight, riders should try, as much as possible, to take some weight down the insides of their thighs, the inside of the knees and the top insides of their calves. This distribution of pressure not only amplifies our aids but lessens the weight stress on the horse's back. It only involves a slightly different, and more helpful, way of thinking on our part.

The right contact

As I said above, much modern, conventional riding seems to be centred around a very firm, unrelenting bit contact which many veterinary and behavioural experts have made clear is distressing for the horses, not only because of the restriction it places on their comfort, ability and action but also the pain and sometimes the injuries that can be caused. I have heard two main reasons for this type of contact. One is that horses need the 'support' of a 'firm, stable' contact to enable them to achieve the balance necessary to perform the movements required of a horse in modern competitions, and another is that horses need to be under good control to be awarded adequate marks to be placed in competition. Anyone who has a reasonable knowledge of equine biomechanics and psychology knows that these 'reasons' do not hold water.

Horses do not balance on their mouths but, as just explained, within their torsos, hence the classical seat. Horses also can be kept under perfectly adequate 'control' by means of correct, highly effective modern training using not only true classical principles but also the rigorously tested and proven techniques of equitation science. Horses are not by nature bombastic control freaks: if they play up or refuse to work as we wish, it is almost certainly either because they are confused and upset by our irrational aid application or because of some other lack of ability to perform, such as pain, discomfort, bad memories of similar situations or lack of strength and fitness to comply.

The old standard of an effective, comfortable contact to aim at is to use just the amount of physical constraint you would use to keep a small bird in your hand without hurting it. Equitation science has a more precise scale of contact pressure running from 0 to 10; 0 being no pressurising contact at all (the weight of the rein) and 10 being as hard as you could possibly pull in an emergency. Level 3 or maybe approaching 4 is regarded as

Figure 6.4: Gadgets of any kind are not needed if a horse is well-trained, and humanely and correctly ridden. They seem to encourage many riders to be harsh because they undoubtedly give them power and are easily misused. They are a sign of uneducated horsemanship and incorrect thinking and attitude. The answer to a horse not going well is to go back in the training and re-school. Inadequate bit education of both rider and horse is a major cause of this kind of situation, plus lack of knowledge of negative reinforcement. (See Chapters 7, 8 and 9.)

'Light' – a fair, comfortable and effective contact. I have found that **many** horses, particularly after a lesson or two in kinder riding than the modern norm, and having experienced a mutually advantageous balance between them and their rider, prefer and go very well indeed on about 2.5 but it is individually decided. I certainly find a level of 4 too much for most such horses.

To find your contact, visualise this scale. What you want is a horse not excessively moving his bit around, happy with it, and certainly not frothing at the mouth which is indicative of a cramped throat (due to bit pressure) preventing him swallowing his saliva. Someone on the ground who understands equine facial expressions (I recommend Dr Sue Dyson's Equine Ethogram – search it online) will recognise a happy, unworried expression on the horse's face. From 0 to 10, apply a 3 contact and ride around, then take it from there, perhaps under a sympathetic, knowledgeable trainer of the classical and/or equitation science persuasion.

Remember that too much contact will always adversely affect a horse's outlook and performance. But too little pressure on an on-off contact due to a just-too-long rein, so that the horse gets a little jab in his mouth at every stride, can be just as bad. Go for what I call a friendly, in-touch contact, keep it stable and reliable but also flexible, and see how you go.

Effective, humane aids

What do we mean exactly by effective and humane? Effective obviously means that our aids get the required response. Humane means that they do so without hurting or confusing the horse. As well as giving aids by means of hands, legs and whip-taps for direction (whips must never be used for punishment or forceful coercion), we can also use our hands and fingers on the horse's body such as neck, withers, shoulders and, indeed, anywhere we can reach. We can use our bodyweight and our voice and, if on the ground, body language or positioning.

Horses are far from stupid but they do think rationally as a prey animal. Both classical riding and equitation science stipulate that we give our aid and then stop giving it **the instant** the horse complies. Extensive research and practice in equitation science also tells us that, to understand whether a horse has responded to an aid correctly in such a way as to stop the minor discomfort of it, such as a squeeze with our legs, a tap with the whip or a 'feel' in his mouth, we must stop that aid within one second of his responding **correctly**.

Horses are lightning thinkers. If we give an aid and the horse tries various actions to try to get rid of the slight irritation most aids produce, we need to keep giving the aid till he gives us the correct response, then stop it instantly. The horse will have learnt, in one trial, what to do to stop that particular feeling. That means that next time you will get a quick, light response. Perfect. Also, the instant he does respond correctly, our releasing or stopping the aid is his reward, perhaps followed immediately by 'good boy' or a stroke, which he will immediately associate with feeling good. It's as simple as that but we need to get our timing absolutely correct.

If we release the aid too slowly and he has been doing something else meanwhile that we didn't want, we have rewarded him, by releasing the aid, for doing that wrong thing. He will link our aid with what he was doing the split second before it stopped, so our timing must be perfect for his brain. It's also no good fumbling in our pocket for a treat to reward him, either, because we'll have missed by several seconds our opportunity to teach him correctly.

That's the basis of training horses by not only modern equitation science techniques but also older, practice-proven classical ones, too. A classical teacher I had in the 1980s used to say: 'Don't keep asking for the salt once you've got it.' Point taken. This all goes for whatever aid you use – hands, legs, seat, voice or whip – the instant it has worked, stop it, and if you want to give your horse an extra reward do so immediately so he links it to his actions.

7

How Horses Learn
And so, How to Train Them

In this chapter:

- ❖ The future of equestrian involvement and training.
- ❖ Explaining equine learning theory how to use it and why you need to.
- ❖ Working with a modern, scientifically proven training scale.

We discussed in the previous chapter how horses think and how to work with their specialised minds. We evolved as hunters, they evolved as prey animals, we approach the world from totally different viewpoints, yet we can develop some wonderful relationships together. We can also mess things up to the point of no return, either by not understanding what we are doing or by doing what some respected 'other' has told or advised us to do.

Both circumstances are understandable. However, I do feel that many of us could pay a little more attention to our own common sense and instincts and simply not continue with what is not working or what feels wrong to us. I know very well how daunting it can be to argue with a well-known, highly qualified and maybe highly recommended trainer on the spot in a school and maybe with an audience.

The fact remains, though, that the horse you are in charge of at that time, whether your own or not, depends on you for his or her welfare and well-being. Many years ago – and I have always bitterly regretted this – I gave a riding school horse a good hiding on the instructions of his owner because of some repeated 'disobedience'. I actually felt terrible but I did it because I was told he was 'just trying it on to see what he can get away with because he's lazy.' (This is a typical human viewpoint but, as I now know, not an equine one.) This instructor was quite highly qualified and, to my eternal shame, I did as she said.

Nowadays, it is known that horses do not think in that way and the findings over recent decades in equitation science have given us a very clear idea of how their minds really work. That does not mean that everyone at that time would have been inclined to hit the poor horse, but it is most noticeable that there are many people around who, as described earlier, do get tough and, indeed, cruel when they are desperate and don't know what else to do. There is also the attitude that we must not let the horse 'win' in an argument, or we'll never be able to do anything with him again.

I once asked a college lecturer why they were not teaching equitation science, or even carrying over the existing management principles and science taught in their classrooms to the horses in their stables, which were kept on very old-fashioned and hard-boiled lines. She told me that colleges exist to fit students for employment, not to revolutionise the horse world, even for the better, which shocked me a bit – I think that's their ethical role. She continued that employers did not want 'some young slip of a newly qualified student' coming on to their yard and telling them how to run it, that they were behind the times and needed to take on the new, albeit proven knowledge. So the college taught the existing ways, merely nodding to new developments to keep the students informed. That is going to be a hard nut to crack.

I am disappointed at the slow uptake in the horse world of the brilliant knowledge coming from equitation science around the world. It is clear to me that some of our major teaching organisations and administrative bodies worldwide are actively resisting taking on the new knowledge which would greatly enhance equine well-being and probably safeguard the future of equestrian sport. The reasons for this are probably, in my view, that it would mean greatly overhauling the teaching syllabus and much of the equestrian knowledge and often erroneous beliefs we have lived and worked with for generations and, as we all know, human behaviour change is a bigger challenge than Everest. It would also cost a significant sum to revamp the teaching literature, the examination content, to retrain and qualify the college lecturers and teachers – and the task of re-educating the general equestrian public would be a thankless one. But, change there will have to be ...

When I first heard about equitation science, I found it hard to get my head round it and bought Dr Andrew McLean's book *The Truth About Horses: A Guide to Understanding and Training Your Horse*, published in 2003. (Dr McLean and Professor Paul McGreevy were the two main instigators of equitation science in its early days and are still very actively involved.) It took me two readings of the book to really start to understand it and realise that this broke new ground. Twenty years later, equitation science continues to develop as more research is done and new truths about horses are discovered. Yet it is still not widely accepted in our ultra-conservative horse world.

In the international equestrian milieu, there is increasing anxiety about the public perception of horse sports in general and, at the time of writing this, there is a very real possibility of their being considerably curtailed if the horses' welfare is not given concrete precedence in future rather than simply being paid lip-service. Equitation science is surely the major way forward – full details of scientifically proven humane and, therefore, ethical ways of training, working, caring for and managing horses are readily available as are academic qualifications. I believe these will have to be adopted by our key equestrian organisations worldwide, both educational and administrative, if equestrian involvement and competition are going to be allowed to continue. It has already been mooted that, if we don't make major changes for the better regarding equine welfare, we shall not be riding horses in twenty years' time.

Equine learning theory – the how and why

A formal definition of equine learning theory is:

Learning theory is an explanation of how students take in, process and use in practice what they learn. (In **equine** learning theory, the students are horses, so ELT explains how horses take in, process and use in practice what they learn.)

Figure 7.1: A dangerous but familiar situation. This rider is more or less out of control because she doesn't know how to deal with a scary object frightening her horse.

Figure 7.2: The remedy. As well as being alert, particularly in public, it is important to keep a look out for anything potentially frightening, so you can be warned. As soon as your horse is ready in his training, teach him shoulder-fore and shoulder-in (Chapter 9). This exercise gives really good control and can enable you to keep him walking on under your firm, calm, clear but not harsh, seat and positioning, past the object. Calm him, but don't use 'good boy' as you will be praising him for playing up. He can still see the object, but this is actually reassuring as he knows where it is. A long-drawn-out 'easy' is useful. Once you **are** past it, then you can say 'good boy' and stroke his neck.

Non-scientists are often suspicious of the word 'theory'. They tend to say that if it is only a theory we don't need to take much notice of it but, in science, a theory is more definite than that. Another definition, therefore, could be: a scientific theory is an explanation of an aspect of the natural world that has been tested repeatedly and proven in accordance with accepted scientific method.

So, training horses in accordance with equitation science, which has equine learning theory at its heart, means that we are training our horses with rigorously tested and proven methods that are appropriate to and that work with horses' brains and bodies, so can be used with confidence in their working and not causing the horses harm. That can't be said of quite a bit of traditional and conventional horse training and riding methods, not to mention their care and management. That doesn't mean, though, that some more familiar principles and practices are not excellent in themselves.

Much in common
I have always been intrigued and impressed by how similar many aspects of true classical riding and equitation science are. We accept that classical riding principles in general go back thousands of years to Xenophon, as mentioned earlier, and over the centuries many very gifted horsemen and women, often with an astonishing affinity with horses, have devised movements, exercises (such as shoulder-in – 'the mother of all exercises'), control techniques (such as inventing bits to go in horses' mouths), ways of sitting (the classical seat) and applying pressures (aids/cues/signals) to horses' bodies to communicate with them, and generally not only enjoy them but make them useful to humans.

The golden rule in both real classical riding and equitation science could well be the doctors' mantra – 'First, do no harm' –

coined, actually, in classical times, by Hippocrates in the fifth century BC. Both aim at humane, appropriate treatment of horses in every way, in management and training/working them. I always feel that equitation science is the icing on the classical cake: it has added an aspect of unarguable certainty to classical riding, plus the advantages of modern discoveries about what is best for and what works best with horses. It does continue to evolve so we must keep up to date in the right way, as we do with human medicine and other things.

A disappearing world

Because of our economic situation in many parts of the Western world today, many long-standing and exemplary riding schools have had to close down and much invaluable equestrian knowledge is being lost. I had the great good fortune to have learnt, from the ages of four years to about fourteen, at one such riding school that was run by a former British cavalry instructor, his wife and her father that taught traditional, real classical principles. I did not realise till after they retired how lucky I was. After the Second World War, the popularity of horse sports gradually grew and grew, national organisations sprang up such as the Institute of The Horse (the forerunner of the British Horse Society and the Pony Club), different equestrian disciplines developed in mainly the Western world with their own governing administrations, equestrian sports blossomed in the Olympic Games and other national and international horse shows and, by the 1960s, it was extremely difficult to find an establishment that taught true classical principles any longer.

In fact, when I bought my own first horse I was told at the livery yard where I kept him that 'we don't ride like that any more' (like I did) 'it's old-fashioned. We do it this way now ...' I didn't like the way they did it and found that they were constricting, tough, uncompromising and not very horse-friendly, even back then, and, in my view and experience, they have become tougher still on the horses in parts of the horse world where glory and money reign.

I have used the expression 'real' and 'true' classical riding in this book because not all trainers and riders who claim to be classical are. They do not put the horses first. They frighten them. They hurt them. They do not use old, traditional, classical principles to obtain their results in a kind but also effective way, as do practitioners of real classical riding and equitation science. They do use forceful methods and do not seem to understand real classicism, or do not wish to take the time, employ the self-discipline or apply the necessary moral consideration to their horses to get brilliant results in an ethical way.

If you go to a demonstration or teacher marketed as 'classical', watch the horses very carefully and note whether they are comfortable, interested, happy, confident, working easily or seem distressed, frightened, struggling, forced and browbeaten or show any other negative quality. Be safely assured, that the latter effects are not real, true classical riding, no matter what the practitioner says.

I have to say that phoney classical people abound, and you need to be prepared for coming across them. There can be fakers in any discipline, so also be willing to spot them and, for the sake of the horses, don't give them your patronage. No matter who they are, what qualifications they have, what prizes they have won, if they are willing to give a horse a hard time they are not the real McCoy. For the sake of our horses, for our own peace of mind and perhaps for the future of equestrianism, we need to use effective, humane methods of dealing and living with horses. Equine learning theory can be relied upon. Real classical methods and the true classical ethos can be relied upon. Be critical, learn what's right and what's wrong, trust your instincts, your worries and your doubts. 'If in doubt, leave it out', no matter what you are told to do and remember that doctors' mantra – 'First, do no harm' to your equine partner. That doesn't mean being weak or indecisive with him, just think twice and always say to yourself 'If I were a horse, how would I like that?'

When associating with horses, particularly when managing, training and working them, we clearly must do so in a species-efficient manner, that is, we must learn how to tailor our principles and practices to horses rather than any other species, including humans. We have already seen that horses do not think wholly like us: therefore, there is no point in our becoming annoyed if they do not react like us to certain circumstances. Management, training and work must be horse-appropriate and horse-friendly.

A real training scale

For a few generations, horse riders and trainers have used as a guide the training scale of the FEI, the Fédération Equestre Internationale, to help them with their training objectives. It has been changed over the years, the following being the current version widely used internationally:

Rhythm > Looseness > Contact > Impulsion > Straightness > Collection.

I think anyone with much experience of riding and training horses can see that this guide is incomplete and not even a scale because it does not progress in a rational way from one logical step to the next, more advanced quality. It starts off with Rhythm and goes on to Looseness, which is fair enough, but then it gives Contact as the next aim which is strange because Straightness would be the next logical quality to aim for. You cannot expect a horse to develop an even contact or find communicating through the bit effective if he is not straight but crooked, and perhaps wandering off line, with his hind feet not following his fore.

The FEI scale then goes from 'iffy' to downright wrong, from my practical viewpoint, by putting Impulsion after Contact and **before** Straightness. Straightness, in practical terms, should be developed before Impulsion because Impulsion develops the horse's muscles due to the extra activity and strength used, but you surely don't want this if your horse is not yet straight because it will make for uneven muscle development, and that will be hard to correct later. Trouble in store!

There is quite some way to go before the horse reaches the final quality on the scale of Collection. For instance, he has to be strong enough to collect by means of strengthening his hind legs and quarters during engagement of those quarters, engagement not being mentioned. Engagement means bringing the hind legs more under the torso to take more weight and, classically and in terms of equitation science, this must be done by the horse himself, not by the rider forcing his weight back via the bit before the horse is ready and strong enough. That way injuries lie.

No mention is made, either, of the horse being on the bit or 'through', in which the rider feels the energy passing from the hind legs, which create it, into his or her hands via bit and reins. Only once the horse has achieved this important 'throughness' will he be able to go on to Collection. And there is no mention of extension after Collection, despite its being required in some dressage tests. Extension is, in practice, Collection with longer strides, not a flat-out trot with flicking toes.

There is a much more rational, rather different and workable alternative **real** scale offered by equitation science, which goes:

Basic attempt > Lightness > Speed control > Line control > Contact > Stimulus control.

You may well be quite unfamiliar with the meaning of these terms, so I'll explain. **Basic attempt** means that the horse has a good try at doing whatever the trainer is asking. **Lightness** (so disregarded these days) means that the horse responds quickly and lightly to an aid or 'stimulus'. **Speed control** means that the horse controls the maintenance of whatever speed the rider has requested, not speeding up or slowing down unless asked. **Line control** means that the horse continues along whatever line the trainer/rider has set him on **and is straight. Contact** means that the horse voluntarily stays 'in touch' with the bit, the rider's seat and his or her legs. More than that, he has now reached the point at which he can, and does, maintain his own posture – head, neck and body – without the rider asking him to. Finally we have **Stimulus control**; the word 'stimulus' means aids/cues/signals, which stimulate him to do something. In this case, the horse is under the stimulus control of the handler or rider, responding reliably, quickly and lightly to the stimuli, only when asked, with all the qualities listed above and in all places and circumstances. Great job done!

You may be thinking that things like impulsion, collection and so on aren't even mentioned but this is fine because they will exist **incidentally** due to the thorough and rational training he has received.

A horse like this is much safer than many horses today because he is more controllable without being browbeaten or forced, relaxed because he knows what's what, and is a pleasure to be around.

8

Handling and Groundwork
Good Companions

In this chapter:

- ❖ Stable manners.
- ❖ Tying up.
- ❖ Holding a horse for attention.
- ❖ Safe, effective handling and leading.
- ❖ The advantages of 'walkies' for horse and handler.
- ❖ Safe and useful lungeing.
- ❖ Considering long-reining.
- ❖ Loose schooling the beneficial way, on the flat and jumping.

Our relationship with our horse on the ground is where our friendship and partnership starts. We can form powerful and wonderful relationships with smaller animals, such as dog, for instance, but we don't sit on them. We may well have bought our horse to ride but the fullest friendship and bond between a horse and a human comes from **being** together in many varying circumstances and ways, caring for him, chatting to him which he soon comes to understand in many ways and helps him to identify us. He will communicate with you through looks, body positions and even thoughts, which you will hopefully become sensitive enough to feel, crazy though some may think this is.

My old Thoroughbred mare, mentioned elsewhere, had her haylage in a large tub in a corner of her box. I was skipping her out once with my back to her when I felt her attracting my attention. I turned round and she was standing by her tub looking at me expectantly. She turned and dropped her head into the tub, then lifted it out again with a 'Well?' look. I went over and found it empty. She then relaxed, knowing I would go and get a refill for her, which I did. She was in exactly the same spot, waited for me to put the haylage in the tub, looked at me, for all the world saying, 'Thank you,' then tucked in.

There is no doubt that horses, immensely strong as they are and easily startled, can seriously injure and even kill us, accidentally or otherwise. It is necessary, then, to create a relationship based on mutual respect along with love or friendship, whatever develops, and for the horse to do as we ask when we are in close contact on the ground. This can be trained humanely from birth, but if you find yourself with a horse that tends to walk all over you, push you around and put himself first all the time, rest assured that he **can** be improved.

My experience with some really difficult horses has shown me that using equine learning theory is a logical and highly effective way of being safe with horses because they soon learn that if they do what humans seem to want they'll get a reward which either tastes good or makes them feel good. As already explained, equitation science learning theory applies to **all** things you want a horse to do, so here, I am going to explain the basic handling and manoeuvring of horses so that they will be, and expect to be, happy and willing to do what you ask – if they can. In other words, they come to trust us. The levels of suspicion visible in horses who have had an upsetting time with us often fall so long as we humans stick to the new rules. To do otherwise is to create yet more confusion and fear.

Equine learning theory works quicker and better than any other training method I have experienced, and in a way that horses find easier to understand than conventional, modern training. Not only does it conform to modern equine science but also it embodies classical principles. We know horses are potentially dangerous animals, mainly because of their inborn flight-or-fight instinct which takes them over in startling situations. A horse in that mode is pretty well uncontrollable but, by sound training to respond quickly, correctly and safely to humane, comprehensible equitation science aids so that he almost automatically obeys them, we can make him much easier and more reliable to control than with less precise methods, and a lot safer.

Four main movements
Basically, we want our horse to do four main things in handling and riding that are important in themselves and form part of all other movements we ask of horses. They are (1) to go forward, (2) to stop, slow down and go backward, (3) to turn the forehand both ways and (4) to turn the hindquarters both ways.

Part of foundation training – the ES term for early training – involves what I have found to be a pretty fail-safe way of training horses to do these things in-hand before they are backed. The techniques can then be transferred easily, quickly and logically to work under saddle, which gives both horse and rider a head start, with horses of all ages, types and roles.

An important point to make is that if a horse has been badly frightened, even after retraining he may revert to his defensive behaviour if that situation arises again and he is scared enough. This does not always happen, a good example being that a horse involved in a transport, loading or road accident **may** load and travel or work in traffic in future without problems.

Handling and Groundwork

Explaining 'reinforcement'

The word 'reinforcement' is used in equitation science to mean strengthening, as in strengthening the likelihood that a horse will respond correctly, quickly and lightly to a particular aid in future. Negative and positive reinforcement are crucial components of good training that horses can understand when applied correctly. They are used in a mathematical sense – 'negative' means subtracting/taking away the contact or pressure (aid), 'positive' means adding something pleasurable such as a titbit, stroking or praising, and 'reinforcement', as explained, means strengthening the likelihood of a correct response in future.

Negative reinforcement

As well as being led, in any method ideally a foal or youngster should be accustomed very early on to being touched all over, feet being picked up and cleaned out and so on, and this can be done with great advantage by using negative reinforcement.

For example, if you plan to start accustoming a foal to being touched, start with his shoulder. Put on his foal slip and lead rope, have the foal near his dam (or, if possible, a friend if an older horse), then place your free hand gently but clearly on his shoulder. If he tries to move away from it, **keep it on his shoulder till he is standing still**, then remove it **at once** (his reward for standing still) and say 'good boy' in a quiet, soothing tone. This reinforces/strengthens the likelihood of your being able to touch his shoulder again in the future and of him standing still. Rubbing the withers or upper shoulder is also a 'feel-good' reward.

Get out of the habit of patting horses because, in horse language, short, sharp feelings are akin to nipping, biting and kicking, and mean 'go away', which is not what you want.

There is a major difference between negative reinforcement and conventional and traditional methods in this task. Horses respond to whatever was happening the instant before they responded. In conventional and traditional training methods, the handler will keep on handling the foal to get him used to the contact, even after he has stood still, all the while praising him but not giving him any reward his mind understands on a practical level. In practice, this is confusing to the equine mentality, and confusion is a major cause of 'disobedience' or, rather, self-defensive behaviour.

If the foal manages to remove himself from your touch, or if you remove your hand while he is still objecting, you will have reinforced his objecting behaviour and he will have learnt that he can escape your touch. Just start again and persevere calmly and patiently. Older horses used to confusing contact with humans can also usually be retrained in this way.

When the foal accepts your touch and you remove it, this acts as a reward and a confirmation that the thing to do is stand still and he'll get some kind of feel-good reward. When you have said 'good boy' you can immediately rub or scratch the foal's upper shoulder where horses mutual groom each other.

Positive reinforcement

This means the addition of something good such as a treat or rub on the withers or shoulder. 'Good boy' can also soon be seen as positive reinforcement. Verbal reward can be given, in-hand, ridden or lungeing, without the need to touch the horse, to reward a correct response to an aid or verbal request, so increasing the likelihood of its happening again. Always reward within one second so that the horse links it to his action.

An important point is to keep all aids/signals/cues as identical as possible so that the horse can rely on the trainer to be consistent. If negative and positive reinforcement are used correctly, and in all handling, groundwork and riding, and an identical vocal reward follows the right response within a second, horses will come to know what to do to remain safe and to get something nice, and get those happy hormones pumping around. Feeling good also gives them an interest in participating in what you are doing.

How to do it

As most people don't have their horses from youngsters, we'll assume a mature horse. Moving a horse backward is an effective control action with most horses and so is a valuable safety practice, on the ground or under saddle. We'll start with that, then continue with moving forward, then turning the forehand and turning the hindquarters, and finally standing still, described as 'park' in equitation science-speak.

Equipment: You need a hard hat/helmet, strong shoes or boots and gloves; a body protector is always a good idea, and you'll need a schooling whip. This is to help in communication and understanding: it is **never** for punishing or causing a horse fear or pain. It is used for guidance and to create minor irritation to ask the horse to move away from it and so relieve himself from that irritation, negatively reinforcing his own action.

Accustom him to the whip's feel by using negative reinforcement, stroking him gradually, gently (but not tickling him) all over his body and legs, keeping the whip on him till he stays still, then immediately taking it off and rewarding, as previously described.

Your horse should wear a close-fitting but not tight, head collar but not a controller-type head collar or one exerting additional pressures. If he is used to a bridle he can wear that, with a comfortable snaffle bit.

Environment: You need a quiet environment so that the horse can concentrate on you. A large, empty loose box is good, with no bedding so he can move easily. An outdoor enclosure is good

Partnering Your Horse

or an outdoor or indoor school. Horses learn better if others are standing quietly nearby.

Procedure: You are now going to train your horse to step backwards in response to a **light** feel via the rope on his nasal planum (the flat bone down the front of his face) or via the reins on the bit. Stand him with his right side next to a wall or fence with plenty of space behind him to step backwards. Stand on his left facing his tail, at almost arm's length from the side of his head. Hold the lead rope so it doesn't hang down, in your left hand about 15 cm/6 inches from his mouth behind his lower jaw. If he is wearing a bit, bring the bridle reins over his head and put your left thumb in the loop at the buckle end to keep them up, then hold the reins in your left hand, like the rope. Hold your schooling whip in your right hand.

To train going backward:

Do not give a vocal aid, or say anything, even if he understands 'back'; just stand still. He has to work out and correctly respond to the pressure aid himself, not to just pay attention to your movements, which he might if you walk in the direction you want him to back up. One tiny step backward is wonderful for now. When you reach the point where you have to walk to stay with him, make sure he moves first, then you follow his movements. Here it is in more detail:

- Pull the rope/reins **straight** backwards towards the underside of his neck, horizontal to the ground, and exert a light, clear pressure on it.
- If he does not step back within two seconds or at least make a 'basic attempt' by lifting a hoof and putting it down a little way back, **don't** stop asking as this rewards him for doing nothing. Increase the pressure slightly and, if necessary, vibrate the aid lightly and quickly, keeping the

rope straight and horizontal to the ground. **Don't** in any way try to push him backwards.

- **Do not stop if he doesn't go back.** Keep vibrating (not jabbing) and now also **tap** quickly, about two taps a second, with your whip on the front of his left cannon, tapping faster if he doesn't respond.
- It is crucial that you continue both these requests till he makes a basic attempt to escape their irritation by lifting his left fore hoof and putting it down again a little way back or actually taking a full step backwards. This might take a minute or even two this first time, but don't stop! If you stop even for a few seconds, you will have rewarded him for **not** stepping back.
- When you get a basic attempt, stop both aids **immediately** so that he learns how to get rid of that irritation, keep quiet, but quickly scratch or rub the side of his withers or upper shoulder as a feel-good reward. Say 'good boy' immediately after you start scratching.
- Now give yourselves a brain-break for about five seconds, then repeat. He will respond quicker this time. Do this three to five more times in exactly the same way, then stand and fuss him or walk him around, head low, for a minute or two before doing a second, shorter set of three to five repetitions. Rest again, then do a third set of one to three repetitions.

You'll find that your horse will gradually improve at this. When he is quite good, introduce the word 'back' as soon as but not before he moves back. He will then associate the command with the movement. You can soon stop using the whip-taps and, eventually, he will go backwards from a single light aid from the rope or rein.

You'll need to repeat all this on his right side with everything reversed but with the same timing. It's best to train on one side in the morning and the other later in the day, or the next day. You can train both sides in one day if you have to. Also, do not ask for more than two full strides backwards, eight footfalls, and only when he is sure about this over time. Never rush or force him, or run him backwards. Short sessions are always better than long ones, and always stay calm, precise and stress-free.

If he takes two strides back you will need to walk forward to go with him **but he must move first**. If you are training in a small area, you will also need to train him to walk forward in the same session. This is not ideal but, if you remain clear and calm, with a full minute break between going backwards and forwards, it is quite acceptable.

To train going forward:

- Stand as before, maybe a little further back, to the front and side of his head. Ask for one step forward. Give the same amount of pressure on your rope or reins **straight forward under his chin**. He will raise his head and poke his nose a little, feeling most of the pressure on his poll,

Figure 8.1: Where to tap – the front of the cannon – to get the horse to step back.

although some in his mouth from the bit. Don't give any vocal aids yet: let him learn one thing at a time.
- Begin with light pressure, increasing slightly if required and, if necessary, vibrate as before – all inside three seconds. On the fourth second, if he hasn't moved, tap his side with the end of the whip where a rider's leg would go, continuing the pressure, vibration and tapping till he takes a step forward. Immediately then stop and rub his withers, following quickly with 'good boy'.
- I find that horses are easily able to transfer these signals to going forward, and usually quicker than when backing. Don't step back yourself too soon in this training: the object is to get him to move to the whip-tap on his side, not to your steps on the ground.

Use the same repetition schedule and train on both sides. Eventually, use very light rein/rope pulls and vibrations but keep up the tapping till he walks, to simulate your upcoming leg aid under saddle.

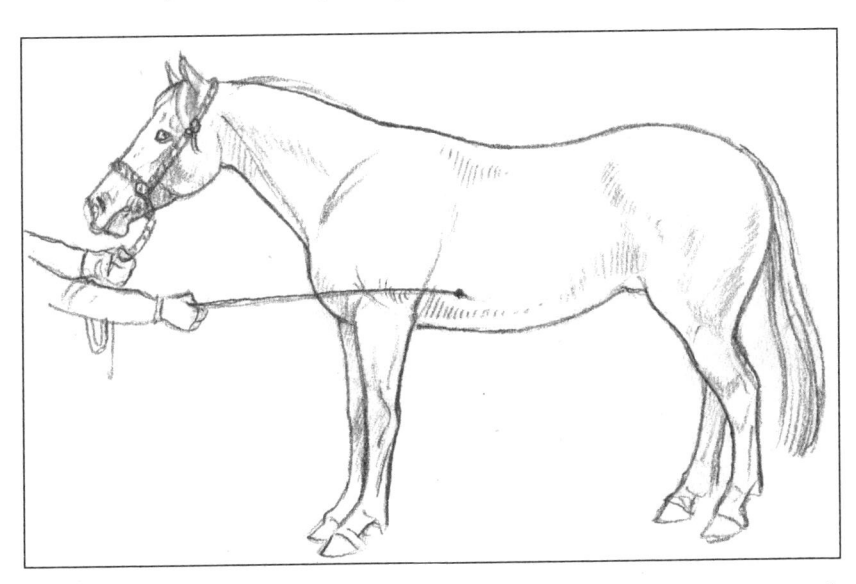

Figure 8.2: Where to tap – where the rider's leg will go – to get the horse to walk forward.

To train moving the forehand to the right:
- Walk forward as usual, on your horse's left side.
- If he is in a head collar with, of course, the rope clipped on under the head, you cannot give a direct turn aid to the right. Instead, pressure the noseband area on the left to push the head to the right by pushing the rope to the right under his lower jaw.
- It helps to tap his shoulder behind your back with the whip, or get a helper to do so, just above his elbow, co-ordinating the timing of your aids. (Incidentally, horses initiate their direction with their forehand, so this will be quite easy.)
- As he will have been led around like this from foalhood, he will accept this quickly, although this method is more precise. Then train to the left.

To train moving the hindquarters to the right:
- Stand your horse in an open space, standing on the left of his neck and with his left hind leg a little forward.
- Start whip-taps on the outside of his left hock to ask him to move that leg under his body to the right.
- As before, keep up the tapping till he moves the leg. It is helpful to bring his head slightly to his left and keep it down a little.
- As soon as he takes one step with his left hind across to the right, even if very small, reward and rest.
- Eventually, ask for more steps, gradually moving the whip aid up to the side of his hindquarters.
- BUT, **never tap forward in the flank area**. It is too sensitive and could upset your horse, causing them to run back and/or kick out.

Train to both sides, of course. You can also introduce the vocal cue 'over' just as he begins to move the leg in the right direction, not before. He will make that link and soon obey your voice.

Handling and Groundwork

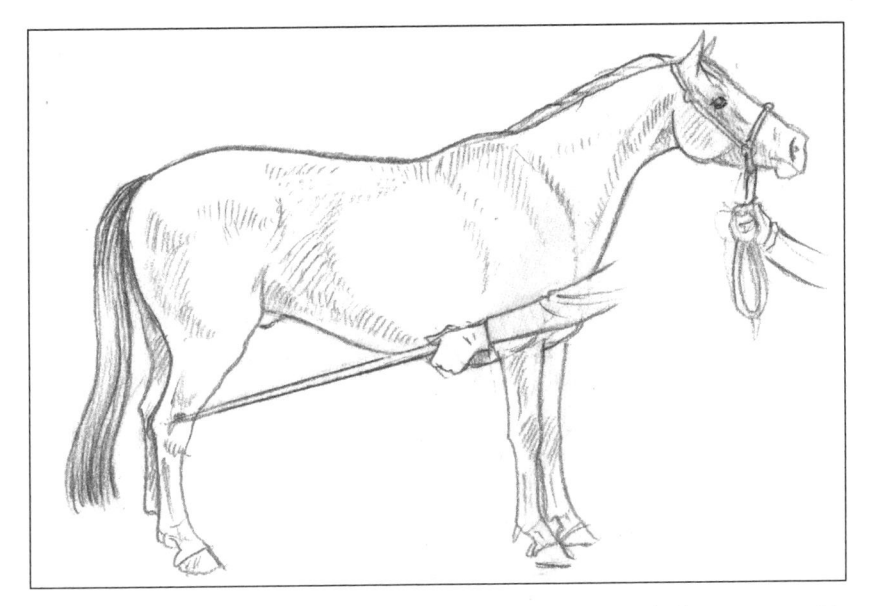

Figure 8.3: Where to tap – the side of the right hock – to get the horse to turn his hindquarters to the left, and vice versa.

A voice from the past
The legendary Australian horseman, the late Tom Roberts, said a horse must **stand** still, not be **held** still. How very true. This is a definite safety feature and is more likely to happen if mounting is not uncomfortable or even painful for the horse. As mentioned earlier, mount, ideally from something high enough for you to step over on to your horse rather than using a stirrup, especially from the ground. It reassures and calms horses when they know they don't have to do anything. Fidgety horses quieten down and they all become more self-confident, in my experience. Remember, though, that if anything sufficiently scary happens the horse will probably move – fast!

To train stand or 'park':
Your horse must be reliable at stopping, going forwards and backwards and, therefore, be familiar with the rein or rope aid and, most importantly, the whip-tap. Your aim is to have your horse

standing until he is asked to move by means of a rope or rein aid, not by following your legs. Many people, including me, believe in the convenience and safety of having horses readily responding to our voice aids. The point against it is, I understand, that the horse might move off if he hears someone else giving a familiar command.

- So don't use vocal aids till your horse is reliable in this work.
- Lead him about in walk, then halt him as trained. Halt your own feet **just after** he begins to stop
- Hold the rope, or put the reins over his head and hold them under his throat. Face him and take one step back. Be sure not to exert any pressure at all on the rope or reins. If he starts to walk forward, immediately tap the front of the cannon on the most forward leg to put him back in place.
- **As soon as** he is standing back in place, rub his withers.
- Walk back again one or two steps, being ready to tap him back quickly if he follows you. He will soon get the hang of what you want.
- Repeat, walking back the length of your rope or reins, if you can, exerting no pressure at all on them and ready to tap him back. Stand him still, rub or scratch his withers, and introduce 'good boy' when he stands still.
- Now try walking from side to side in front of him. He will watch you so be ready to correct him, if needed. Eventually, if he doesn't move, walk all round him on both sides as far as the rope will let you.
- Before long, you will be able to run round him from hip to hip in both directions. He might think you are crackers but will not move a foot. Confirm this training in other safe places.
- If you want him to obey 'stand', say it when he is good at this and as soon as he halts but not before. Then rub his withers at once, saying 'good boy'.

Teaching a horse to stand to a voice aid can be a lifesaver if he gets loose somewhere he shouldn't. To train this, say your chosen word as soon as he stands still straight after you have tapped his cannons, so he can link the vocal command with standing still. Whenever you want him to stand, use it, but tap him back if he moves. He will soon become 'classically conditioned', or used to, standing still till you tell him to move.

Because you have trained him only to walk off in-hand, after standing, to a forward-pressuring rein or rope cue – no vocal aid such as 'walk on' – he will be much safer than most horses to handle. However, you will need to tell anyone else who cares for him how to do this, otherwise your horse will become confused and worried. Many people chatter to horses and other people while working around them and it may be difficult to get them to understand that this is not appropriate for your horse, and might cause problems.

If you do want him to learn to walk forward to your vocal aid, don't choose 'walk on' because most people do and, as explained earlier, he might walk on if he hears someone else say it. Choose a different sound, keep to it and tell his other handlers. Train him to obey it by saying it as soon as he walks, not before, so he makes the association.

Think like your horse

I have used this method of starting horses off or retraining others for many years and know that it really works. We need to learn to think more like a horse rather than expecting them to almost read our minds. We need to work in a more structured and precise way to apply equitation science methods, but it results in noticeable improvements in equine welfare, confidence between horse and owner, increased safety and, because the horse can trust and understand us, greater well-being for him. That's what it's all about.

General 'good behaviour'

This section covers stable manners, being tied up and holding a horse for attention. Having gone through the equitation science method of handling training in this chapter, you will, if you are consistent, have no problems with your horse complying with good, basic manners, which is necessary for safety.

When you want to enter your horse's box and start to slide the bolts back, he should stand back and make room for you, stand still and allow for your movements without hassling or rushing you even if you are bringing food, let alone squashing you or disregarding you. With the handling techniques explained, and a good response to vocal commands such as 'back', 'stand', 'over', 'up' (for feet) and any other simple sounds you want to train, plus consistency from you, he will be a good host to you in his domain where, otherwise, he can do just what he likes.

Being tied up is important and a good way to train it is with a head collar and a lungeing rein. Thread the lungeing rein, clipped to his head collar, through his tie ring and hold the free end in one hand. Ask him to back, if he is close to the wall. If not, ask him to walk on, saying 'stand' before he quite reaches the wall. If he backs away, bring him back with the rein, saying 'walk on', quickly followed by 'stand' again, and reward him at once. Repeat this till he can be safely tied up while you work around him. The next step is to do this in a safely enclosed outdoor space, and make this routine a habit **every time** you go into his box until it is second nature to him. Never take his obedience for granted. Be meticulous about your timing and rewarding.

Holding a horse for attention is usually best done in a bridle, although horses trained as above should be safe to handle in a head collar. Do not stand directly in front of him holding one rein at each side as this is not safe; he could easily toss his head in your face and injure you. With your in-hand training, especially obedience to 'stand', he will normally fall into that routine and be good to work with. It's usually safer to have a horse in a box or enclosed space, when possible.

Being good to handle and lead is also a great help if, when, you take your horse for 'walkies' to get some grass when grazing is restricted, or just a change of taste. Horses, I find, love little trips like this and the closeness really cements your relationship. You can have a break like this during a long ride, or lead him out anyway as a way of spending extra relaxation time with him. He might need to wear an appropriate sheet or rug depending on the weather, and, being well-trained in hand, should be fine in a head collar. Grazing out in public spaces, though, calls for a bridle with a comfortable, jointed or lozenge snaffle bit so he can graze and swallow in comfort.

Lungeing your horse

Lungeing is not part of equitation science training and most people do it badly, dangerously and leaving the horse with a bad impression of it. However, it is a common technique in other schools of thought. The main two faults are having the horse go too fast and using too-small circles. Both these can frighten horses, be very difficult for them and ruin their opinion of not only lungeing but of us. If you do want to lunge, or do any work like long-reining or loose schooling, fit protective boots to your horse all round and, for lungeing, I advise a strong, sturdy lungeing cavesson that will not slip round your horse's head, rub his offside eye and offer very little control. In fact, discomfort can hype a horse up and is counter-productive and dangerous.

Lungeing reins are the length they are for a very good reason – they allow the horse to move comfortably on a shallow bend, particularly if the trainer is prepared to intersperse going round and round by walking for some distance on a straight line. It does accustom a horse to dismounted work and answering vocal requests, and good work can be achieved in getting a horse to follow a curved track, to use his body freely (lack of gadgets permitting), raise his back, lower his head and develop his physique and balance.

It takes some practise to handle the rein in one hand and the long whip and thong in the other, so you can use a driving whip if you like, to encourage the horse by pointing it at his hindquarters or slowing him by pointing it in front of his head. Twenty minutes is adequate for lungeing, ask your horse to walk out well, trot slowly to moderately and, when he is used to this, to canter calmly and **not** at all fast.

Your body language, like your whip, can direct your horse. Your horse will be watching you and react to your body and whip. If you want him to lower his head, he probably will if you bend down a little, if you stand level with his forehand he will probably slow down and if you stand level with his hindquarters he will probably speed up.

All in all, change rein/direction frequently, do a little more on his not-so-good rein and finish on a good note on his better rein. Keep everything calm and too slow rather than too fast and always reward good work instantly with 'good boy' – or 'good girl', of course.

Long-reining is not as popular as lungeing, partly because it demands more skill and partly because the trainer has to do as much work as the horse! It is, though, much more versatile and useful than lungeing. I cannot do better than recommend two little books by Sylvia Stanier, *The Art of Lungeing* and *The Art of Long-reining* to gain really expert, realistic advice on how to become proficient.

Loose schooling
I have never met a horse who doesn't like loose schooling, provided the trainer doesn't overface him with difficult jumps – and you don't have to ask your horse to jump, of course.

Handling and Groundwork

Jumping loose is safer and more controllable if you construct a lane, perhaps from poles and fence supports, or whatever safe equipment you can get, so that the horse feels free but not entirely so.

You need to train him thoroughly in voice commands first, especially whatever you use for slowing down and stopping! To start off, lead your horse in a relaxed walk down the lane, then trot him, perhaps over a few poles on the ground to create interest for him. The first time he goes down loose, walk with him on the other side of the lane and progress from there. An indoor school is obviously the safest and most convenient environment and many riding centres, including colleges, will rent theirs out for a given time and/or give you a lesson in how to proceed. It is good fun for you and your horse; brings him on in his work and makes a change from his normal work.

9

Flatwork

From Going Backwards to Galloping

In this chapter:

- ❖ The purposes of traditional school movements.
- ❖ Training and riding basic school movements.
- ❖ Balance and technique at different gaits.
- ❖ Hacking alone and in company.
- ❖ What to do when.
- ❖ Gauging progress and moving on.

Humans probably first started using horses for domestic heavy work such as transport and farm work, once farming had developed. Very early civilizations, having been used to hunting them for food, started keeping them contained in fenced-in areas for convenience, and started using them for not only meat but also blood, milk, hair and hides. Driving is believed to have come next, for the transport of goods and people, initially using vehicles such as **travois** or with runners on sledge-type vehicles, rather than wheels. Once wheels were invented, people never looked back. Wheeled chariots were developed for warfare, various carriages for general transport of people and goods appeared, and riding seems generally to have developed last of all.

Early peoples were well aware of the advantages of looking after their bodies, including exercise and general movement for getting and keeping fit. It is not unreasonable to suppose that they fairly soon applied this idea to their horses. In particular, ridden horses used for warfare had to be strong, fit and agile, and people with a leaning towards horse development and fitness must have been intrigued to devise exercises to improve their way of going and their ability to get their riders out of trouble on the battlefield.

The earliest recorded text on horse development and management for war was written by Kikkuli on four clay tablets in 1345 BC when he was horse master to the king of the Hittites. He got the horses in his care amazingly fit and included swimming in their schedule, although some of his ideas sound strange to us today. Nevertheless, his cavalry and use of fit, strong and usable horses enabled the Hittites to rival ancient Egypt as a power to be reckoned with.

Xenophon, the ancient Greek cavalry commander mentioned here already, who lived over the period of about 430 to 355 BC, wrote a book still famous today – *The Art of Horsemanship* – which contains much wisdom and instruction still of great value today, including recommending kindness in handling and training horses. It could well be included with advantage on examination reading lists today.

Nearer to our time, François Robichon de la Guérinière, 1688–1751, was a Baroque era French horse master and author. His book *École de Cavalerie* or *School of Horsemanship* has been a bible for many people in and after his time, and it is still probably the most famous horse book in the world. He was the inventor of the 'shoulder-in', known as 'the mother of all exercises', as a suppling exercise for horses.

I thought you might like to know all that, but what has it to do with riding, and reading, today? Reading and studying old books can offer us salutary lessons in how important horse and man have been to each other over the many centuries they have been together. True, we would look askance at some of the methods, beliefs and practices of old, but it is true that modern riding does not have a monopoly on kindness. In fact, in some areas of the horse world it seems to be in very short supply. Older ideas, true stories and methods put it all into perspective and expand not only our knowledge but also our own panorama and frame of mind where horses and our relationship with them are concerned.

The purposes of school movements

The various airs, or movements, we see if we watch famous schools of riding might entertain us or startle us but, very often, people can see no use for them today. It's true that some of the more extreme airs above the ground might seem pointless or even asking too much of obviously cosseted horses, but they all had a purpose in warfare in evading or attacking an enemy horseman, or even a soldier on the ground.

The airs that are used in dressage competition today, or rather their original versions, might still impress us but many people still don't know what purpose they serve. As stated earlier in this book, most of the exercises we ask of an educated, trained horse are for the specific purpose of making the horse stronger, fitter and more agile when ridden. When done correctly and with some understanding of equine biomechanics, they do achieve this purpose.

Unfortunately, today the original ethos of developing a horse to be able to give the best of his **natural, individual** abilities under the weight of a rider and his or her accoutrements often seems to have been thrown out of the window. The moves we see in general equestrian competition today are, to older-school horse people, actually potentially damaging to the horses. They are often greatly constrained and/or hampered by their riders on the flat and over fences, their gaits much exaggerated, their efforts to jump blocked, with some horses often clearly struggling and showing signs of distress, anger and pain to those who know what to look for. Many observers find that even the FEI rules as to ways of going, devised to protect horses, are ignored, apparently by the FEI itself.

In this book, the work and exercises I detail at a basic level are well within the capabilities of any reasonably conformed, healthy horse and will do him nothing but good when done correctly. Owners and riders, however, will find great benefit in working with the help of an approved classical and/or equitation science trainer, and details of both the organisations having details of such trainers are given at the end of this book in the section 'Help and Information'.

Training and riding basic school movements

Here we'll talk about walk, trot, canter, gallop and an introduction to lateral work with leg-yield and shoulder-fore and shoulder-in.

The walk, as described earlier, is a four-beat gait with the feet falling two on one side then two on the next – left hind, left fore, right hind, right fore. In your relaxed, balanced, classical seat, you will feel the back swinging, dipping and rising on one side then the other. Your seat now will not hinder your horse's movement at all, being relaxed and much more accommodating to his movement than previously, so he will probably, naturally, walk out comfortably and freely. As the left side of his back dips your seat bone on that side will dip down and forward with it, then rise up and back as the right side of his back dips in its turn. You will not allow your shoulders to rise and dip also and disturb your horse because your upper body is held erect but not stiff and all your horse's movement is absorbed from the waist downward. Your seat, stretched up from the waist and dropped down from the waist, is soft and relaxed as are your legs, supported in the stirrups with the balls of your feet on the treads. Because your legs are dropped down with your ankle joints directly below your hip joints, you don't need to push your knees and heels down: they will drop down naturally.

Your horse's natural walk is almost effortless for him, especially if you sit in this non-interfering but supporting way, going with him. Your contact can be on a level 3 contact on the equitation science scale of contact pressure, which keeps you in touch but without giving your horse a worrying, over-firm pressure in his sensitive mouth. Some horses, though, go well and feel better on a little less than 3, so do try that.

In walk, your horse's head rises and falls with his stride and also swings a little from side to side, some horses and ponies doing this more than others. A sensitive rider will allow for this within the contact, not by moving his or her arms backward and forward both equally with the movement, which does not take account of the slight swing, but by keeping her elbows in place by her hips and slightly opening and closing the fingers accordingly. When the head swings down and left as the left forefoot lands, the left rein will feel a little looser and the right one correspondingly a little tighter. To avoid an alternate, uneven feel in the horse's mouth, the left fingers need to close slightly to take up the slack and the right ones to open slightly to reduce the tightening feel, and vice versa. This movement is very subtle but it is important for the rider to follow and allow for it, opening and closing the fingers just a little as the horse's head swings naturally and slightly in accordance with his back and leg movements. Horses really appreciate this extra thoughtfulness on your part and bring themselves 'together' more for a regular, beneficial walk action.

So you are going with your horse's walk actions with your seat and your hands, and he will be comfortable, walking on in harmony with you which promotes his confidence. This kind of walk keeps you in touch with each other and a horse can walk on for miles in this way. If you let him walk out on your hacks or in your school, say during your warm-up, with a good seat movement but on a long rein, your horse's back will not rise slightly beneath you and his hind legs will be strung out somewhat behind. Riding all the time like this can cause back problems because the back's natural arch will be flattened a little due to the weight of you and your saddle. Loose rein walks are fine for short periods, but a gentle but meaningful contact, as described, keeps your horse more 'together' and brings his hind legs just a little more underneath him, raising the back into its stronger, slightly arched posture. This protects it under your weight and is an ideal walk for basic work and hacking, which we are considering in this book. Horses who go always with a slack, dropped back never develop their back and neck muscles and look strung out rather than evenly developed and together.

To ask the horse to walk from halt or to walk on a little faster, give your leg aid with your inner calves **inwards** and slightly release with your fingers.

To turn or follow a curve in walk, put your inside seat bone and shoulder forward a little and perhaps weight them a little **without** tilting over in that direction. Slightly open your outside fingers and perhaps tighten our inside ones a little, depending on your feel on the reins. If you need to give the horse a bit aid to turn, slightly close the fingers on the side to which you want to turn, allowing this by slightly loosening the fingers of your outside hand. Pressing the outside rein **sideways** against the horse's neck will help the turn (remembering that horses use their forehands to change direction). If you feel you also need an outside leg aid to help the turn, use your outside leg inwards just a little forward from its normal position. To change direction in walk, just reverse these aids and, obviously, straighten up for a straight line.

To halt from walk, stop moving your seat with his back movements and keep your hands and fingers still. This will usually be enough to bring him to a halt up to the bit and standing more or less square, at least in front.

To move up to trot from walk, be ready to shorten your reins a little because the head will be naturally more up and in trot and will be still rather than swinging. Take your upper body slightly forward from the hips, not the waist, keeping your back flat, and give a single squeeze with your calves, taking up the rise as he trots. Keep your upper body forward like this, your shoulders over your knees: this will enable you to perform the movement described below very comfortably and minimally, with easy control.

In the classical rising trot, the seat movement is far more subtle than the conventional one of up and down. Instead of fully rising, rise only very slightly and just tilt the lower part of your pelvis forward, then let gravity take you back again in time with his rhythm. So you are thinking 'tilt, sit, tilt, sit' rather than up and down. This keeps you closer to your horse with no disturbing thrusting up and down. Keep your hands quite still and maintain your even contact on your slightly shorter rein, because in trot the horse's head does not swing with his stride.

The 'sit' part of your action will be when the outside hind and inside fore are coming forward in the air. With a horse used to a rider doing things correctly, simply changing your sit and 'rise' or tilt to the other diagonal is often enough to get the horse to change direction. However, if you are trotting on a long, straight lane or track, you should change the diagonal frequently to prevent your horse's body developing unevenly and to avoid problems in trot on the other rein.

To halt from trot, stop the tilt phase and sit in the saddle, also bringing your upper body upright. Give a gentle but clear, even feel on the bit and assume your walk action, then give the halt aid.

[illegible] bout the horse's back [illegible] during it, the [illegible] on the side [illegible] e right side [illegible] **To take up** [illegible] seat bone [illegible] ner calf of your outside leg, slightly back, trying to make it w[illegible]n that leg is in the air. Because the right side of your body is slightly forward, though, horses know what's coming (even if you or the horse have never done it this way before, I find!) and canter much more readily, correctly, with this powerful but subtle body positioning, even if you get your timing wrong. You can look in the direction you want to go, whether that is to the right or straight ahead, and maybe give a slight right-rein aid, although this is not always needed. Obviously, to canter left reverse the aids.

To trot from canter, just bring your seat bone and shoulder back level with your opposite ones and your horse will trot because he is less comfortable. There is no need for a feel on the bit; the seat repositioning is enough. Conversely, canter work is so much easier when the gait is acquired in this way because it conforms to the positioning of the horse's back. So many problems in canter occur because the rider has not positioned the appropriate seat bone forward, usually because his or her teacher doesn't know about it.

For fast canter or gallop, you will need slightly shorter stirrups than usual so you can adopt a balanced, light seat with your shoulders, and probably your elbows, above your knees, which are above your toes. There is no really noticeable transition from canter to a faster canter, which is still three-time, or gallop, which is four-time, as described previously. The horse's head goes significantly back and forward in gallop and you have to use your arms appropriately. Do keep in touch with his mouth, though, and don't get so excited that you lose contact and flap your arms all over the place. Even though competent race jockeys do this ostensibly to encourage the horse to go faster in a 'driving finish', I think this is human thinking, not equine, and the horse would be much more comfortable and confident, and perhaps therefore go faster, if his jockey kept as still as the gait allows and in touch via the bit.

The canter stride double footfall (the second beat of the canter) splits, so the forefoot lands a little later than the hind which accompanies it in canter. Horses can readily do a flying change in gallop to change legs when the muscles used in, say, right canter become tired, so they change to left canter to rest them and use the other lead's muscles.

Figure 9.1: Horse and rider in a fairly fast gallop, often called a hand gallop. The rider's hands are moving forward to accommodate the horse necessarily stretching his head and neck forward in this phase of the gallop, without becoming over-enthusiastic and flapping the arms and hands about and unbalancing the horse.

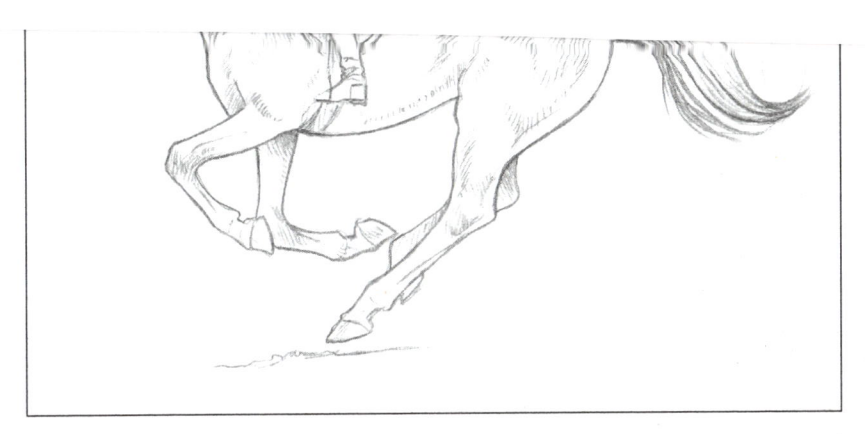

Figure 9.2: The hand gallop again; the next phase with the rider's arms and hands coming back during the moment of suspension. This forward-back action in fast gaits helps keep a consistent but flexible contact in the horse's mouth, maintains in-touch, mutual communication and does away with the unpleasant, common, jabbing action of an erratic contact.

To slow down in canter or gallop, raise your upper body very slightly and give a slow-down, halt aid feel on the bit, plus whatever voice aid you usually use to steady or slow your horse. The good, old English 'whoa' given in a long-drawn-out way, or a singing 'wo-ho', is very familiar to most horses, especially if they feel that your heart is no longer in their fast gallop! This combination of requests will work unless your horse is well over-excited and, let's face it, most of us get literally carried away at sometime.

(Another good thing about equitation science is the subtle but effective control it gives you, which is so reassuring anyway but especially when things are getting hairy-scary. It becomes reliable, consistent and habitual, and horses, in my experience, are much calmer and more biddable when they are used to living with its powerful and almost irresistible influence. They know what to expect, they know they can understand us, I think they feel that they are being fairly treated and, all in all, these states of being promote good mental and physical health which is better for both of us.)

Rein-back: A correct rein-back is not as difficult as many people make it look, with horses squirming and swinging around, hind legs splayed and obviously arguing with their rider. Rein-back is a fairly advanced movement in practice, but it is important to be able to get your horse to step backwards for manoeuvrability and safety reasons, and it's no big deal. It doesn't have to be 'dressage correct'.

Come to a halt with a slight lifting of your seat and a closing of your fingers on the reins. Now, keeping your seat light, maybe with a fractional leaning forward to help, give a gentle but definite feel on the bit – **no leg aids** because legs mean forward and this is the main problem – confusion. Your legs can be passively back a little to guide the hindquarters. If a single feel on the bit does not work, maybe because your horse is not used to this, give it again and vibrate it slightly, keeping it up till he goes backwards. Then stop. (Negative reinforcement.) When he has done the required few steps, stop the bit aid. He should stop there and then but if he doesn't give a gentle hint with your legs. He may not be used to this but will relieved at not being asked to go forward and back at the same time, and will soon catch on.

Basic school movements

If you can school/train your horse to have good basic paces and be obedient to your aids, you will be doing better than very many riders. As a teacher, I find that the main problem with most horse-and-rider combinations is one of attitude on the part of

Figure 9.3: Rein back. Often badly done in dressage tests, here the rider is asking rather than hauling on the bit, which is very common. The bit aid should be one gentle but clear ask after another, repeated at the rate of about two per second till the horse takes a step, or more, backwards. The equitation science in hand work will have taught him to respond lightly to this. Many well-trained horses subsequently take their cue from the rider's slightly lightened seat, step back to one squeeze and continue till the rider signals otherwise by resuming the vertical seat, when the horse will usually halt. For walk-on the rider gives an inward squeeze of the legs, not hampered by bit pressure which could feel like halt to the horse and so cause confusion.

Here the horse is slightly behind the vertical. This is not because the rider is pulling him back but because horses often do this naturally when stepping backwards. You can easily tell the difference, when watching, between free will and force. Here, the rider's upper body is slightly forward to help lighten the seat and make raising the back and stepping back easier for the horse. Her legs are slightly back, still and passive, guiding the hindquarters into a straight, backward direction. It is amazing how many riders squeeze with their legs in rein back, when horses have been taught that that means 'go forward'. This results in hauling on the bit, the horse squirming backwards and swinging the quarters, plus raising the head as the horse fights against the rider's increased bit pressure to counteract the leg aids! What else can the horse do?

the rider which rubs off on the horse, horses being so sensitive. This adversely affects their relationship and the horses know it, but cannot know why. Many riders are anxious that they are 'no good' and feel, anyway, that they don't really know what to do when they go into the school for a schooling session without a teacher present. In lessons, they often try to impress the teacher while apologising for not being very good. Others suffer more from slight anger, blaming and complaining about their horse all the time.

In the first case, the teacher should try to find out why the rider has so little confidence and it's usually because they don't know how to fix their own problems – that's what teachers are for, anyway. In the second case, if a horse is seen to be at fault all the time, it is nearly always because he doesn't understand what his rider wants, is uncomfortable or in pain when ridden or has no confidence in him or her. Any good teacher will try to put horse and rider at ease, try to get to the root of attitude issues, and get the basics right before trying anything more complicated.

The gaits having been discussed, let's talk about basic school movements. If we ride in a school we are bound to be going round in circles to some extent; circles, that is, not potatoes.

One of the most famous classical teacher-trainers in the world, Nuno Oliveira, who trained my own main teacher, was talking to a young man who was starting to train with him. The maestro asked him if he could ride various movements such as half-pass, pirouette, flying changes and suchlike, to which the answer was always 'yes, of course'. He then asked the young man if he could ride a perfect circle. The young man looked slightly puzzled but said again, 'but of course, maestro'. Oliveira said to him: 'In that case you are very fortunate. I have been trying all my life and have not managed it yet.'

and greatly helped by our seat), interested in his work, obeying our aids, cues or signals, and not throwing us off unless we deserve it. If you have a healthy, sound horse in comfortable tack that fits and is appropriate for him, you are off to a great start. A horse cannot concentrate on training if he is uncomfortable, in pain or anxious.

Another advantage is to break the common habit of looking down at your horse's head and neck most of the time you are riding. We're all prone to it. Someone once told me that horses can 'feel' this and it puts them off, making them feel harassed. Have you ever had that feeling down the back of your neck that someone is staring at you, you turn round and they are? It's a similar thing. Looking where you want to go is a major, major advantage to any riding operation because horses seem to be able to know this, and take it as normal communication. Try to get into that habit instead.

Keeping your horse going: Very many people need to keep kicking to keep their horse going. Keep your horse together on your in-touch contact, with leg aids only when needed, maybe to keep him in a regular gait or to make a change. The reason most riders have to kick and kick to keep their horses going is because they have been taught to use much too heavy a contact, so the horse is being told to go and stop at the same time, which is clearly impossible. Just use the ES level 3 contact or less but stay in even, flexible touch and set your horse off. He'll be pleasantly surprised and will keep going, probably with gusto. Horses like moving!

Here are a few ideas to try, with or without your teacher.

Circles: A good way to master circles is to imagine them on the ground and, yes, look ahead about a third of the way round your circle. I'll bet your problems will stop right there. If your horse falls out of the circle, weight your inside seat bone to bring him back, without leaning over and in. If he falls in on the circle, weight your outside seat bone, again without leaning. To encourage bending along the circle, just keep a slight inside rein feel. You can also hold your outside rein sideways on the neck to guide his forehand, with your outside leg slightly back, touching his side but still. Keep him, which will be easier now, in a steady but purposeful gait and do your perfect circle!

Corners: These tiny parts of a circle can be quite useful in schooling. As you approach your corner, say you want to go left, put your left seat bone and shoulder forward a little (like cantering) and give a gentle feel on the inside, left rein. That will do it, but you could also have your right leg back a bit and your right, outside rein pressing lightly against his neck/shoulder region.

Loops: Shallow and deeper loops down the long sides of an arena are good ways of suppling up horses, teaching them about 'bend' and avoiding the boredom of continual straight lines. At first just come in from the outside track to the inside track, the deepest part of the loop being at the middle of each side, where you will change bend. Take loops seriously, simple though they seem. Keep your horse walking on, progressing to steady trotting. You are on a continually changing bend if you also do a short loop on the short sides. When you can canter loops comfortably and correctly you are really progressing!

Serpentines: Serpentines can be [...] across the school or, the more modern way, as [...] across the school with semi-circles at the ends, fitting at first three down a 40 m-long school but progressing to four. These, like most school figures, aim to get you and your horse thinking, performing bends correctly but with a 'rest' on the straight lines.

Figures of eight: Two circles meeting at X, figures-of-eight are a standard school figure and can be pretty testing, which is why they are used so much. The correct way is to start at X and do a circle on one rein, coming back through X and doing one on the other rein. Sounds simple but two accurate, pure circles on a continual bend can be quite taxing to both horse and rider. The ultimate aim is to do them in canter with a flying change at X. Good luck.

Squares and diamonds: These are quite useful for teaching your horse, and yourself, to start turning corners in a turn-on-the-haunches way. As we've said, horses take up their direction of travel via the forehand so naturally take their weight back a bit, which is always a good exercise for a riding horse. If you are doing a square, two of its sides will have no support from the school fence or wall and you will have four right angles to describe. If you are doing a diamond, in a 40 m x 20 m school you make your shallow angles at E and B and your sharp ones at A and C.

To make your turns, your horse should be amenable to turning his forehand for a few steps under saddle. Approach where you want to turn, slow down somewhat and turn the horse's forehand mainly by weighting your inside seat bone and pressing your outside rein on his neck. Your inside rein can ask gently for inside bend (no pulling his head round!) and your legs keep the gait going.

Leg-yield: Leg-yield is used to introduce lateral work to the horse. It is not so demanding as, say, shoulder-in because body-bend is not required. The conventional way to do leg-yield is to walk in a straight line, say down one of the quarter lines or even just the inside track if new to this, to ask the horse to go sideways towards the outside track. The rider asks for slight bend of the head and neck **away** from the direction of movement. The sideways aid is given by the inside leg, slightly back, pushing the horse over towards the track, while the other leg keeps up the momentum of the gait. The outside seat bone (on the side to which he is moving) is weighted slightly which makes the lateral aspect easier to obtain.

Another way to do this, which I prefer, is to perform leg yield without the bend of the head and neck. **With** the bend, horses are inclined to go in a diagonal line, shoulder leading, towards the track, which results in virtually no lateral movement, and this can be difficult to correct. With what I call straight leg-yield, this distraction, in my view, is avoided and the lateral aspect is more likely to happen easily.

Shoulder-fore and -in: Here we have that 'mother of all exercises' because it does require bend and is the horse's introduction to all other true lateral work. It is best first learnt on the track. Have your horse walking smartly up to the bit, put your outside seat bone forward a little (directing your horse still up the outside track) and press your outside rein sideways on his neck/shoulder area. You only want **slight** bend for now, to get shoulder-fore before the full shoulder-in.

The difference between shoulder-fore and shoulder-in is that shoulder-fore is not angled quite so much away from the track, the horse's bend is less and his hooves form four tracks, whereas in shoulder-in the forehand is angled in slightly more, the bend in the horse's body is a little more marked, and the horse's hooves form three tracks. Imagine watching the horse from the front, the four tracks in shoulder-fore are, working inward from the fence, outside hind which is still on the outside track, outside fore, inside hind and inside fore. The three tracks in shoulder-in are outside

Figure 9.4: The footfalls in shoulder-fore. All four hooves are visible from the front, with very slight but adequate 'bend' in the horse. In shoulder-in, the horse produces a little more bend and there are three tracks rather than four. (See text.)

hind on the outside track, outside fore which is in front of and obscuring the inside hind, and inside fore.

There is a temptation to pull the horse's head in with your inside rein but this will only produce bend in the neck and probably too much. Use your outside rein as described and just give a feel on the inside rein to obtain slight bend in the neck, in towards the middle of the school. This amount of bend in head and neck will be sufficient for shoulder-in, too: your outside rein will direct the shoulders in more to achieve more bend in the whole body.

Shoulder-in is your key opening the door to the more advanced lateral movements, which presumably you will share with your teacher.

What to do, when

Your basic work is to have your horse obeying your aids. Performing your simple, basic work very well is much better than trying more complicated moves and making a mess of them. Get straight lines, large circles following the correct bend and track, manoeuvrability and general co-operation sorted first. More difficult work such as smaller circles, deeper corners, lateral work and so on are based on good preliminaries, so make sure your foundations are in place before trying to do anything more demanding. A 10-metre circle is much more difficult than a 15-metre one, for instance.

If you ask too much you will feel your horse struggling and you will not achieve your aims. Don't be too demanding of your horse: find a good teacher with your outlook on equestrianism and work with him or her. Progressing too quickly, hitting your horse, jabbing him in the mouth, kicking him particularly with spurs on and using force rather than reasonable pressures never produce good results and are not horse-friendly.

When you are getting good results you will be able to feel the ease with which your horse performs his work. He will not struggle, he will not 'argue' with you and he will not produce sub-standard work. If he does you are asking too much at that particular time. Step back a bit to easier work, work at that level, and not every day or for more than, say, forty minutes, and try to move up a bit in a few days' time or the next week. Your horse's condition and future performance will be your confirmation and reward.

Hacking, alone and in company

The traffic conditions on our roads and the deteriorating manners and dangerous behaviour of many drivers make hacking much less of a pleasure than it used to be unless you can access traffic free places. Here in the UK, our Highway Code has increased protection for horse riders and other similar vulnerable road users, but it is still a definite must to give a horse traffic training, to wear high-vis clothing and to have your horse under good control near traffic. Hacking alone on a horse good in traffic is acceptable if you are careful where you go, but only a lunatic would hack on a horse who is not reliably good in traffic.

Riding alone, just you and your horse enjoying the wide-open spaces, is wonderful but you have to be realistic. Wear high-vis, put high-vis on your horse, take your charged-up phone and carry ID. Attach ID to your horse's saddle, too, in case he gets loose. Riding in pairs or small groups is safer if not always so enjoyable. The same common-sense rules apply to all members of a group, and the well-behaved horses can protect and teach the others.

10

Jumping

Forward to the Past

In this chapter:

- ❖ Jumping seats and techniques, past and present.
- ❖ The effects of them all on the horse.
- ❖ Taking a jump the horse-friendly way – helping, not hindering.

I want to use this chapter to persuade readers to think again about using the modern jumping seat. It seems to be everywhere in the horse world, in my view very much to the horses' detriment.

The common picture is of a rider presenting his horse at an obstacle, the horse spots it, gauges his effort, adjusts his stride and just at the moment of take-off when he needs full freedom of his head and neck to make his effort and adjust his balance, his rider pulls back on the reins to haul himself up the horse's neck, thinking perhaps that he is helping him. This completely blocks the necessary use of the horse's head and neck which need to stretch fully out and over the fence. Instead of arcing smoothly over the fence the horse has to lurch himself up and over, straining his back and experiencing significant pain in his mouth as the rider pulls himself up via the bit and blocks the horse's natural movement, also unbalancing him. The rider will then, during the flight, lean on his hands which are propped firmly on the crest of the horse's neck, gripping the reins. This prevents the horse stretching out his head and neck which he needs to do to balance and have freedom during the flight part of his jump.

On landing, riders can often be seen to bang their seats back down into the saddle instead of staying up and slightly out of it to give the horse freedom to rebalance and get away to the next fence, where the process will be repeated.

The reason for this jumping technique, I believe, is because riders in general are not taught today to acquire what is called 'an independent seat', one which does not need the rider to use the reins to get and stay in position or even on board. An independent seat used to be the jewel in the crown of horsemanship but is rarely seen today. Riders may stay on board but it is through contrary, forceful methods which seriously hamper the horse's faultless, natural jumping technique.

I understand that strain and work-sustained injuries are more common today than when a more harmonious rider position and technique were used, and horses suffer more mouth injuries which is not at all surprising. The fences today may be more technical, cross-country and in showjumping, and not so high and wide in general, but horses' careers seem to be shorter, and perusal of photographs, film footage and live audience viewing show, it seems obvious to me, that riding techniques are not so accommodating of horses' physiques and natural movement.

Earlier jumping seats

The most innovative and surely humane jumping position ever devised is that developed by Federico Caprilli, an Italian cavalry officer, horseman, teacher and author whose life spanned the nineteenth and twentieth centuries. He was the inventor of the forward jumping seat which revolutionised the lives of horses and their riders. His book *The Caprilli Papers: The Principles of Outdoor Equitation* fully explained the forward jumping seat and much more about horsemanship. His seat is still the basic foundation of the modern jumping seat although, as always happens when anyone tries to improve on perfection, today's common seat is the worst offshoot of it so far. Anyone jumping in today's fashion would never be able to descend on horseback the near-vertical drops of the Italian cavalry of Caprilli's time or clear with ease **and no interference with the horse** the horrendous obstacles taken for granted in his time.

Before Caprilli, it was common to be taught to approach jumps in an upright position, swing the upper body forward on take-off, or even remain upright, and lean back on the descent with the legs forward so that the horse's back received a tremendous thud of weight via the stirrup bars as his forefeet hit the ground and the full weight of the rider, plus the force of his descent in the saddle, shot up the leathers. His mouth was no better treated as his rider would use the reins as an anchor during these acrobatics with, apparently, no smidgeon of consideration for his sensitive mouth or a passing thought for the intense pain the horse suffered. And in those days such riders commonly rode in curb bits.

Although not all riders were that bad, most were. Classical riding was mainly applied to riding on the flat but there were a few enlightened, compassionate folk who applied classical principles to the pioneering seat devised by Caprilli, who was, in essence, an unheralded classicist. An illustration of classical principles applied to jumping, with an unmissable nod to Caprilli, appears in this chapter, with informative caption. This type of seat, taught widely in the early and mid-twentieth century, gives the horse all the consideration and freedom he needs during jumping.

Objectives of 'classical' jumping

Classicism is a set of humane principles that put the well-being of the horse first while achieving high standards of equitation. Equitation science has identical aims and results, promoting communication methods that horses understand and producing superb performance as a result. It so happens that, by working with these joint principles, horses definitely perform better because they are not afraid, they are confident, and they work in freedom. Their minds, bodies and spirits are catered for and because they feel safe they thrive and their health is better. We could not wish for more. So let's take a closer look at a far superior jumping seat to the one usually seen today. It is based on the mutual, matching balance of horse and rider with its increased safety and security, non-interference with the horse, and economical use of energy and strength because it allows the horse to use his naturally evolved jumping action. This humane and effective jumping seat has been thoroughly tried, tested and proved in international competition over decades and is readily available for everyone to use, to the benefit of both partners. Our horses deserve no less.

The development of an independent seat means that the rider does not rely on the reins for support so does not hurt the horse's mouth or restrict him.

In the approach the rider folds his torso down from the hip joints while also pushing his seat back and down towards the cantle. His chest is above the horse's withers, not up his crest, so he is close to his body and centre of balance.

On take-off the above position is maintained, the rider's hands do not ride up the horse's crest but stay low and forward, permitting the horse his full, necessary freedom.

During the flight the torso stays low and the seat back to maintain the mutual balance, the hands follow the horse's mouth down and forward on an extremely light or free rein, indeed ideally allowing the mouth to take them down. The lower legs stay down and close to the horse's sides.

In the descent and landing the seat is purposely kept out of the saddle to prevent banging it on the horse's back via the saddle. The rider raises his torso and takes up a light bit contact as the horse raises his head for the getaway.

Figure 10.1: The classical jumping seat. In the approach the rider sits in a light, balanced seat, with the angle of balance shoulder > elbow > knee > ankle. As the horse lifts off for the flight, she does **not** throw her body and hands forward and up but adopts the correct, helpful balance of seat **back** to the cantle, upper body folded from the hip joints **down** to the withers/lower neck, and hands, **down and forward** to the mouth, which enables the horse to stretch fully in the take-off to start his arc over the fence.

The take-off is the point of the jump at which hind limb, hindquarter and back injuries are likely **if** the rider hampers the horse's action by throwing herself up his neck and out of balance and, most commonly, significantly restricts his head and neck by supporting herself, gripping the reins of course, on the crest of the horse's neck, effectively stopping him using his head and neck in their essential 'balancing pole' function, which is out and forward. (This can be seen in any jumping class worldwide.) The horse has no choice, therefore, but to lurch himself over the fence by means of unnatural biomechanical and muscle use, likely to injure him.

Jumping

Figure 10.2: The flight. The all-important free and full stretch continues to be enabled by the rider maintaining a close body contact, correct balance and total 'give' in the reins. It is, in a nutshell, seat back, torso folds down, hands down and forward.

Figure 10.3: The landing. The freedom of the horse's jumping action, with classical techniques, enables him to land smoothly one leg at a time which is much less injurious to the tendons and ligaments of his front legs.

During the getaway the rider keeps this position with his seat out of the saddle to help the horse get back into his stride, then resumes his between-jumps seat, whether that is a light, forward seat or a more upright one.

This seat is appropriate for all jumping situations, including racing, with possible adaptations for very high fences. The rider may well need, in that case, to raise his torso in line with the horse's neck in, for instance, puissance classes but the basic principles protecting the horse's comfort and welfare, particularly in his mouth, can be catered for by fitting a neck strap in case the rider, as is quite possible, needs to hold on to something.

Forward to the past

Jumping in the classically based seat described above is a revelation to someone used to the modern one. The rider is closer to the horse in mutually felt balance, moves around less, accommodates the horse's needs more and the pair are generally more successful because of the increased comfort, the saving of energy and effort and the increased smoothness of performance. An elderly, retired veterinary surgeon whose main practice was with jumping horses once told me that when this seat was common there were fewer stress-and-strain injuries to horses in general, fewer mouth and dental injuries from the bit and far fewer back and hind quarter problems. It is clearly so much kinder and safer all round for horse and rider that I fervently hope it will be revived, partly because of the increased public scrutiny of the equestrian world but mainly, of course, because of the welfare and well-being of our precious horses, who make it all possible.

Epilogue

If you have read this book from its beginning to here, I thank you for your time and attention. There are so very many horse books to choose from, and horses themselves continue to be irresistibly popular in our lives, even in these exceptionally hard times, that it is a compliment to me that you have chosen this one to read.

The point of the book is to emphasise something many people often overlook and that is that making a more equal partnership of our relationship with horses is not only good for horse and human but also has benefits in our mutual enjoyment of each other, our activities together and how we feel about each other and, therefore, it increases our well-being and our mental and physical health. It's healthy to be happy, we know now.

The horse world has always had a general culture of us humans being superior to our horses insofar as they have to do as we wish and we are in complete control of their lives – indeed, of whether and when they are born and die. Some people still speak and think of them as 'servants' – 'he's been a good servant to us' – yet so many of us genuinely think of our horses as our friends. Maybe they don't sleep on our beds or luxuriate in front of our fires in winter but good friends they can certainly be.

Even so, we talk of 'training' or 'schooling' our horses to get them to do as we want. Is that so bad? Children sent to a decent school are trained, along with their academic lessons, and taught social niceties and mores, good manners, things you can do and things you just can't, so there is no reason why we can't do it with our horses, our dogs and, so far as is possible, any other animals we have around us.

Our horses also subtly train us, too, don't they? We acquire a horse and put all the basics in place such as buy bedding, horse-type food, tack so that exercising him is easier, keeping his stable clean and his grazing fit to eat, and we encourage him to mix with other horses to make friends and create a life of his own with them. But, after some time has passed, we start to realise that he needs other things and attentions personal to him. He may make these obvious to us like eating or refusing certain foods, demanding freedom and the company of friends, expecting us to fulfil our routine, or changing the routine if it doesn't suit the horse. These things may cause us inconvenience or expense but we provide them because he needs them. In other words, we also treat him according to his individual traits and quirks, we accommodate his whims and we go out of our way to provide the kind of lifestyle that makes him, as an individual, happy.

Not everyone does those things, of course, and many horses live a depleted life, a life of imprisonment, loneliness, discomfort or pain, and fear of the humans who are supposed to care about them. In those cases, the horses really are servants or, even worse, slaves.

The point of my writing this book was to try to present a less common way of associating with our horses, one that would be rewarding to both of us, one in which our horses would understand that we want in many ways to be equal to them, caring friends who do not always expect to get their own way, but who are happy to acquiesce to their needs and wants whenever we can.

Epilogue

I hope I have managed to get my point over and illustrate the benefits of a much more equal partnership than most horses and their 'owners' enjoy, and how to create it. A lot of it lies in our attitude to our horses. They are not underlings! Because horses do not have a hierarchical society like ours, perhaps we could start with considering their viewpoints more and how they live together, and take a few cues from their attitudes to each other and to us. We can only gain a more rewarding relationship, friendship and, yes, a true, give-and-take partnership.

Books to Trust

The books listed here are specifically chosen to take further the topic of being a partner to a horse. They all promote the right, humane, thinking attitude to horses and horsemanship although, of course, their authors may have differing personal views. Where possible, when sourcing books it is always good to find the most up-to-date editions, often with accompanying DVDs and websites, so that you have access to the latest information.

Barbier, Dominique and Liz Conrod
Broken or Beautiful: The Struggle of Modern Dressage is one of an increasing number of books calling attention to what very many horse people, it seems to me and including me, see as the sorry state of much modern horsemanship. A most pro-horse book to guide, inform and reassure all who want to do right by their horses, clarifying why some common practices are bad for horses (yet still widely taught) and others beneficial. Don't miss it.

Caprilli, Federico
The Caprilli Papers, Principles of Outdoor Equitation, by Captain Federico Caprilli, translated and edited by Major Piero Santini. A

detailed explanation of the development of the forward jumping seat plus much more. Describes a truly horse-friendly way to ride jumps.

Draaisma, Rachaël
Language Signs & Calming Signals of Horses: Recognition and Application
A fascinating and enlightening book about horse communication, psychology and partnership. I learnt so much from this original and unique book. Highly recommended.

Heuschmann, Gerd
Tug of War, Classical versus 'Modern' Dressage: Why Classical Training Works and How Incorrect 'Modern' Training Negatively Affects Horses' Health, with DVD. Second edition. The author is a veterinarian and horseman. This is his first book and he has since written several others which can be sourced online. Essential reading for anyone who cares about horses.

McBane, Susan
Please forgive me for mentioning four of my own books. *Fine Riding* is my first book to cover equitation science with true classical riding. Two books which complement each other and are popular with readers are: *Revolutionize Your Riding* (which concentrates mainly on the horse) and *Horse-Friendly Riding* (which concentrates mainly on the rider). Finally, *Conformation For The Purpose* is a detailed, accessible guide to conformation and action for different equestrian activities.

McGreevy, Paul
Equine Behavior, Second edition. A very comprehensive treatment of its topic by one of the key instigators and practitioners of equitation science worldwide. Important and eye-opening.

McGreevy, Paul, Janne Winther Christensen, Uta König von Borstel, and Andrew McLean
Equitation Science, Second Edition. Indispensable for anyone wishing to get up to date on modern knowledge and attitudes. Non-scientists should not be deterred from reading it: there is an excellent index and enlightening glossary for further helpful references and down-to-earth help. If you really want to understand and help your horse, I advise you to buy this book.

McLean, Andrew and Manuela (of Equitation Science International)
Search online for used copies of the first edition of *Academic Horse Training: Equitation Science in Practice,* a sizeable hands-on how-to book on the principles of ES and how to apply it, in detail. A second edition is in preparation. **Essential reading.** Search the Shop at Equitation Science International at www.esi-education.com/shop/ where you'll find several other key books, 'real' and digital, plus other invaluable products.

Podhajsky, Alois
The Complete Training of Horse and Rider still every true classicist's bible decades after its first publication, by the former head and Director of the Spanish Riding School. Pure classical principles from initial handling to airs above the ground, plus a clear, deep love of horses. Also search his other books; *The Riding Teacher* is particularly important today.

Skipper, Lesley
Lesley is a friend, and colleague on *Tracking-up* magazine (*see* 'Help and Information' next). My favourite of her several books is *Let Horses Be Horses: A Horse Owner's Guide to Ethical Training and Management,* which should be required reading for

examinations. Search her several other books for sound common horse sense and no-nonsense language.

Wilson, Anne
Anne is also a friend and part of the team on *Tracking-up* magazine. Her book *Riding Revelations: Classical Training from the Beginning,* is a very detailed, easy-to-understand book to put riders of any level on the right road to effective, humane riding. A really encouraging read that lets you know that you can do it!

Other important authors to look for on our theme: Marthe Kiley-Worthington, Sylvia Loch, Tom Roberts, Sylvia Stanier.

Help and Information

Sources of information, education and interest, presented in alphabetical order:

Association of Pet Behaviour Counsellors
The APBC is an international network of experienced and qualified pet behaviour counsellors who work on referral from veterinary surgeons to treat behaviour problems in horses and other animals. APBC members are able to offer the time and expertise necessary to investigate the causes of unwanted behaviour in animals, and outline practical treatment plans that are suitable for their clients' circumstances. For further information, visit *www.apbc.org.uk*

Classical Riding Club
The international Classical Riding Club, founded by probably Britain's premier classical rider and teacher, Sylvia Loch, is no longer active but its website is still available, with its invaluable archive of many hundreds of articles freely accessible to all. It also features the CRC Trainers Directory listing classical trainers all

over the world by name and by location. Find out more at *www.classicalriding.co.uk*

Equitation Science International

Equitation Science International is the education wing of the Australian Equine Behaviour Centre, founded and run by Andrew McLean and his wife Manuela. In my experience, their staff, also, are most efficient and helpful. ESI's stated mission is: 'to educate horse riders and handlers in equitation science to enable efficiency and safety in all horse interactions.' They offer various educational opportunities online and 'live', including the accredited and highly regarded Diploma of Equitation Science, a horse training and coaching qualification that provides a full understanding of horse training and is appropriate for all equestrian disciplines and activities. Enjoy browsing their site, shop and practitioner list at *www.esi-education.com*

Human Behaviour Change for Animals

As any teacher knows, the most difficult part of teaching people in relation to their animals is to get them to change their behaviour towards them and to use more effective methods in their dealings with them. HBCA specialises in this skill. It operates internationally, runs a consultancy, is involved in research and organises training sessions and events both live and online. Visit its website at *www.hbcforanimals.com*

International Society for Equitation Science (ISES)

Probably the most important equestrian organisation today – my opinion. The ISES is a non-profit organisation that 'chiefly aims to facilitate research into the training of horses to enhance horse welfare and improve the horse/rider relationship'. It is a membership organisation, with various membership categories open to people with appropriate qualifications and experience.

However, non-members are also welcome to attend its annual conference, with often ground-breaking presentations, held in a different country each year. ISES sells its wedge-shaped taper gauge to individuals and organisations, to be used for gauging the appropriate fit, as regards tightness, of horses' nosebands: the gauge also measures the circumference of bit mouthpieces, to check compliance with FEI rules. It issues periodic position statements on matters of importance in equine training, management and welfare. Its website, which I regard as essential reading for all equestrians, is at *www.equitationscience.com*

The Saddle Research Trust
The Saddle Research Trust is a charity registered in England. It aims to 'promote the health, welfare, safety and performance of ridden horses and their riders'. It has a strong educational ethos, with freely available, open-access, web-based resources and e-newsletters – no membership is needed. Its regular public conferences present essential developments in equestrian topics related to the health and welfare of horses and riders. Find out more about their crucial work at *www.saddleresearchtrust.com*

***Tracking-up* magazine**
Tracking-up is a non-profit, voluntary, quarterly, equestrian magazine, available internationally, which concentrates on true classical riding, equitation science, and ethical horse-care and management methods. It is available by subscription or single-copy purchase, in print or digitally. In order to maintain its independent view and to enable it to say what needs saying on behalf of horses, it has no commercial or sponsorship connections. Its editor is the author of this book, Susan McBane. If you drop her an email at horses@susanmcbane.com she will send you full details of how to acquire your copies. You will be most welcome as a *Tracking-up* reader.

Index

Akhal-Teke 24
Andalusian 97
Arabian 24, 97

Barb 97
basic attempt 130
basic school movements 150, 153, 162
bedding 61, 63, 64, 137, 178
behaviour 12, 43, 65–6, 76, 102, 105, 123, 134, 136, 146, 169, 184–5
behind the vertical 100, 161
bits 77, 81
body language 34, 36, 102, 106, 108, 119, 148
Boots 85
breathing 47, 69, 78, 100
bridles 75, 77, 80
British Horse Society 127

canter 55, 83, 92–6, 113–14, 116, 148, 153, 157–58, 159, 164, 165
Caprilli, Frederico 171, 180
centre of balance 82, 92, 173
characteristics 11, 19, 21, 30, 91
circles 54, 147, 162–8
classical riding 17, 30, 78, 104–5, 120, 126–8, 181, 186
classical seat 108, 112
climate 19, 21, 23
cobs 28, 66
cold-blooded 97
colic 56, 59
collection 129, 130
contact 27, 36, 38, 51, 61, 76, 80, 82, 98–9, 104, 110, 115, 117, 118–19, 129, 130–6, 154–9, 163, 174–5
controlled relaxation 111–12, 114–16

corners 164
Cregier, Dr Sharon E. 77

danger 10–11, 22–3, 26, 30, 55
de la Guérinière, François Robichon 151
diamonds 163, 165
diet 22, 26, 55, 56, 57, 58, 67, 71
digestive system 26–7, 29, 56
distressed 39, 41, 128
domestic 25–6, 35–6, 49–51, 54–5, 60, 91, 150
double bridles 81
Dyson, Dr Sue 119

emotions 31–2, 37, 40, 70, 102–3
engagement 130
environment 13, 19, 20, 39, 64, 137, 149
equids 22, 24
equine behaviour 35
equine biomechanics 16, 84, 117, 152
equine communication 43, 45
Equine Ethogram 119
equine learning theory 121–8, 133–4
equine nutritionist 56–7
equipment 30, 78, 149
equitation science 30, 47, 78, 104–5, 107, 117–28, 130–7, 145–7, 153–61, 181–6
ethical 122–3, 128, 186
evasions 99
evolution 20, 25, 27, 29, 30, 55

farrier 72, 74
fear 34, 37, 39, 107, 134, 137, 178

FEI 129, 130, 153, 186
feral 29, 35, 49, 55, 70
figures-of-eight 165
fit of a bridle 79
flight path 92
flying change 95, 158, 165
foals 29
forage 29, 55–8, 63
force 34, 77, 99, 102, 140, 161, 168, 172
forward jumping seat 172
freedom 28, 35, 43, 48, 52–4, 65, 103, 116, 170–8
friends 48, 49

gadgets 77, 148
gallop 11, 21, 25, 26, 55, 83, 92, 95, 98, 116, 153, 157–9
girth 75–6, 79, 82–4

hacking 51, 52, 155, 169
head carriage 42
health parameters 44
herd 11–12, 23, 35, 49–50, 56, 65, 92, 105, 107
Hippocrates 127
horse management 27
hot-blooded 24, 97
humane 119

Iberian 97
impulsion 129–30
independent seat 171
instincts 22, 34, 121, 128
instructors 37, 107
International Society for Equitation Science 17, 80, 185.
inter-species manners 44

Index

jumping 8, 22, 45, 52, 83–4, 90, 96, 108, 110, 116, 132, 149, 170–6, 181

Karabakh 24
Kikkuli 151

lameness 66, 71–3, 92
laminitis 28, 41, 56–7, 73
leg-yield 165
Lesage, Commandant Xavier 90
lightness 130
line control 130–1
Lipizzaner 97
long-reining 54
loops 163–4
loose boxes 28
looseness 129
lungeing 54, 132, 136, 146–8

mature 23, 137
McGreevy, Professor Paul 123
McLean, Dr Andrew 123
mental development 25
mental health 55, 61, 100
modern riding 30, 89, 90, 98, 115, 152
moods 31, 43–4, 47, 66
moving forward 137, 158
muzzle 39, 41, 78

negative reinforcement 118, 135, 137
nosebands 78, 80
numnahs 88

Oliveira, Nuno 162
overweight 57, 66–7

paddock paradises 65

pain 26, 34–42, 72, 74–5, 78, 80–4, 94, 99, 100, 102, 117–18, 137, 153, 162–3, 171–2, 178
partnership 9–12, 14, 45, 76, 102, 107, 132, 177, 179, 181
pasture 26
pelham 81
personalities 13, 30
physical features 24
physical health 48, 50, 102, 160, 177
Pony Club 127
position of trust 31
positive reinforcement 135
prey animal 10, 20–1, 120–1
Przewalski 24
psychology 12, 16, 117, 181
pulse 47, 66–8

qualities 19, 20, 32, 98, 131

rehabilitated 101
rein-back 160, 163
reinforcement 135–6, 160
relationship 9, 13, 30, 45–6, 54, 74, 107, 132–3, 147, 152, 162, 177, 179, 185
reward 45, 58, 120, 133, 135–6, 139, 142, 146, 148, 169
rhythm 129
rising trot 83
Roberts, Tom 143, 183
rugs 85

saddle 25, 75, 76, 82, 83, 84, 88, 99, 108–12, 134, 137, 141, 155–6, 165, 169, 171–2, 174, 176
saddle pads 88

saliva 42, 78, 100, 119
scale of contact pressure 118, 154
seat 25, 82, 83, 95, 104, 107, 108, 109–17, 120, 125–6, 131, 153–81
serpentines 165
shelter 24, 53, 65
shoulder-in 125–6, 151, 153, 163, 165–8
skin 24, 40, 46–7, 67, 78–81
sleep 11, 23, 34, 40, 177
snaffle bits 81
social contact 27, 28
social licence to operate 15, 78
space and movement 27
Spanish Riding School 97, 182
speed control 130–1
squares 165
stable manners 146
stabling 27–8, 61
standing still 67, 135, 137, 145
Stanier, Sylvia 148, 183
stereotypical behaviours 26, 43
stereotypies 58, 101
stimulus control 130–1
straightness 129, 130
survival 20, 22, 55

tack 44–5, 75–7, 101, 163, 178

tail 24, 37, 39, 40, 68, 86–7, 115, 138
teeth 38–9, 45, 50, 70, 81
temperature 46, 67–8, 73
tethered 28
Thoroughbred 24–5, 58, 90, 97–8, 133
training aids 83
trot 55, 73, 83, 92, 94, 100, 112–13, 130, 148–9, 153, 156–7
turning the forehand 137
turning the hindquarters 137
turn-on-the-haunches 165
turnout 10, 27, 50–4, 74, 85
urine 71

vertical position 112
vices 26, 43, 58
walk 12, 46, 55, 65, 72, 83, 92–3, 107, 110–13, 133, 138–49, 153–7, 161, 166

warmblood 97
water 29, 58, 60
welfare 35, 122–4, 145, 176, 185–6

Xenophon 77, 126, 151